The Story of the
California Look
VW

The Story of the
California Look
VW

by Keith Seume

H&S
Herridge & Sons

This book is dedicated to Mark Herbert
(1959–2006)
"Just raising hell and having fun..."

Credits: *No project like this can ever be undertaken – let alone completed – without the help of others. I cannot thank the following people enough for their help and support, be it by unearthing dusty photo albums, telling tales over a cold beer, or posting stories on Internet forums (where would we be without the Internet?). In no particular order, my sincere thanks go to Jim "Sarge" Edmiston; Dean Kirsten; Stephan Szantai; Doug Mische; Ron Fleming; Jim Holmes; Bill Schwimmer; Glenn Gaskey; Mark & Paul Schley; Ken Jevec; Art Alvarez; Mike Johnston; Mike Mahaffey; Suzy Herbert; Jere Alhadeff; Roger Grago; Greg Brinton; Rick Meredith; Mark "Fred" Kessenich; Doug Haydon; Scott "Worm" Blaydes; Mark Ramirez; Todd Fuller; Dave Dolan; Rich Kimball; Greg Aronson – and everyone else who has offered me their time and support. I must also extend my gratitude yet again to Gwynn Thomas for her patient subbing and proof-reading.*

Published in 2008 by
Herridge & Sons Ltd
Lower Forda, Shebbear,
Beaworthy, Devon EX21 5SY

Reprinted 2009

© Copyright Keith Seume 2008

Designed by Ray Leaning

ISBN 978-1-906133-08-5
Printed in China

CONTENTS

FOREWORD

It's hard for me to believe, but over 13 years have passed since the original book California Look VW was published, and in that time we have witnessed an amazing upsurge of interest in the origins of this, the purest form of customising ever to grow out of the Volkswagen scene.

In those 13 years, the one question which I must have been asked a thousand times was "When are you going to do a follow up book?". It seems that people on both sides of the Atlantic couldn't get enough of the subject. Well, I can assure you, it hasn't been for the want of trying on my part, for I've been collecting photographs and stories for several years in the hope that I would find a publisher willing to take on the project. I even considered publishing a book myself, until I realised what a major task that would be. And then, towards the end of 2007, I met up again with Charles Herridge, who published the original book. We discussed a number of possible titles, but there was one which I felt I simply had to do – and here it is!

The new book differs from the last in that there is a greater emphasis on personal stories – you'll read tales of street racing, alcohol-induced tomfoolery, camaraderie, war, music and even a little politics. You'll also see how the California Look developed over the decades, from the use of simple bolt-on modifications to become a technologically sophisticated style which has gathered a worldwide following.

The first book has become known in Cal Look circles as "The Bible" – if that is the case, then this must be "The New Testament". Read on to find out more about the California Look – from Genesis to Revolution…

Keith Seume
Lostwithiel
Cornwall
May 2008

Chapter 1

A DECADE OF CHANGE

"Lifelong friendships and love formed while I had that car – and those are things you simply can't replace..."

1960s

By the end of the 1950s, the Volkswagen Beetle had become a world leader, both in terms of sales and reputation. It was a cheap car, but reliable and, above all, charismatic. Despite a shaky start when it was accused of being Hitler's baby, the Beetle won over the hearts of the American people – people more used to driving chrome-plated, befinned Detroit iron. It spawned a generation – or rather, successive generations – of hardcore enthusiasts devoted to enjoying the People's Car experience to the full.

With their comparatively affluent lifestyle and apparent love of all things glamorous and exciting, it is perhaps something of a surprise that Californians took the humble Beetle to their hearts. But take it they did, with California becoming one of the most successful markets (along with the more cosmopolitan New York) into which the Beetle was sold.

But why the fascination? It would be easy to assume that, following years of wartime austerity (although what the USA endured paled into insignificance alongside what European nations had been forced to suffer), the American people would prefer to drive domestically-produced automobiles, with their V8 engines, air-conditioning and electrically-operated gadgetry. Nothing said "we're doing OK" better than a new Chevrolet Belair sat in the driveway...

Despite this, the Beetle won over the hearts and minds of the post-war baby-boom generation, appealing to a collective desire to be different and to swim against the tide. In the

1950s, Volkswagens were purchased by thinkers – by the 1960s, they were being bought by kids who wanted (perhaps unknowingly) to make a statement.

The rise to power, and the subsequent assassination, of President John F Kennedy was proof enough that America was on the verge of a whole new era in its history. Kennedy was the first president to appeal to a younger generation – and someone who was seen as a threat to long-held conservative values. Kennedy – JFK – became President on 20th January 1961 and would be cut down by an assassin's bullet on 22nd November 1963. His short term in office and the events that followed proved, as if proof was needed, that America would never be the same again.

This turning of the tides was reflected in the music of the era, too. With the obvious exception of the rock and roll movement, popular American music of the 1950s was largely dominated by crooners, singing songs of love and happiness. Nobody sang of war or rebellion – save for the blues movement, where any political statements were largely driven by racial tensions in the Deep South. The first signs that changes were afoot came with the founding of the Motown Record Corporation in 1960, a Detroit-based (hence "Motown", short for "Motor Town") company founded by an African-American and which gave black musicians their first opportunity to spread their music to a wider audience. Not all of American society was ready for this, but there was to be no turning back.

*One of the best-written books of its time, Henry "Hank" Elfrink's **All About The Volkswagen** covered a wide range of topics, including tuning. (Author's collection)*

With its chromed Porsche-style offset rims and dummy "knock-on" hubs, this early EMPI demonstrator is fairly typical of cutomised VWs in the early- to mid-1960s. (Glenn Miller)

In Europe, a new sound was making waves – the Mersey beat, spearheaded by four smartly-dressed young men by the collective name of The Beatles. Their unique sound turned the British music industry on its head – the lead-, rhythm- and bass-guitar-led harmonies were unlike any popular music that had gone before. Heading up the UK charts with songs such as *Love Me Do* and *Please Please Me*, The Beatles soon became the benchmark by which all groups around the world would be judged.

Although they hit the big time in the UK in September 1962, when *Love Me Do* reached number 17 in the pop charts, it would be another 18 months before what became known as Beatlemania crossed the Atlantic. On 9th February 1964, The Beatles appeared for the first time live on American TV on the Ed Sullivan Show – newspaper critics called them a passing fad, but record sales soon proved otherwise. As Bob Dylan's third album, released in January 1964, just ahead of The Beatles' visit to the USA, was to proclaim, times were a-changin'…

In the same year that The Beatles made their mark on American youth culture, President Lyndon B Johnson (LBJ) turned his full attention to the affairs of a country about which few American people had ever heard: Vietnam. For over a decade, there had been tensions between the Communist-ruled northern territories and the more liberal south – a division along the 17th parallel that had been agreed under the terms of the Geneva Convention in 1954. JFK had already shown his support to the South Viet-namese government by creating a joint US-South Vietnamese air force, using American pilots, and by sending in the Green Berets.

When LBJ came to power, he further committed US military resources to the region by giving orders to send USAF planes to South Vietnam. That was in January 1965. Two months later, 3500 ground troops were sent to the region – by December that year, there would be over 200,000 US troops in Vietnam. It was the start of a conflict that would have a far-reaching effect throughout American youth – VW enthusiasts included.

However, on the drag strips of the west coast of the US, there were other battles to be won. The first of the so-called muscle car wars were being fought, as manufacturers tried to outdo each other in the pursuit of performance. Ford launched its mighty 427ci Thunderbolt engine, while Mopar unveiled the legendary 426ci Hemi. Installed in otherwise relatively mundane mid-sized sedans, these engines turned the performance market on its head. Other manu-facturers followed suit: Pontiac came up with the GTO, AMC the Rebel, while Chevrolet squeezed its big-block 396ci motor into the Chevelle. Following a marketing campaign that was akin to trying to persuade a teenager to buy a Magnum revolver for target practice, these tyre-shredding monsters were available straight from the dealer.

Yet, despite the ready availability of such machinery, there would always be those people who relished the challenge of taking a rather

Dean Lowry is considered by many to be the godfather of VW performance tuning. He was among the first to uncover the potential of Volkswagen's air-cooled flat-four engine. (Dean Lowry)

Lowry's own race cars, each named Deano Dyno-Soar, were front-runners in NHRA H/Gas competition. Note the lack of roll-bar and the huge steering wheel! (Dean Lowry)

more prosaic vehicle and turning it into a dragon slayer. As we shall see, there were relatively few performance parts available for the Volkswagen at the time, so head-to-head competition was out of the question – it would be difficult to win the muscle car wars in a tiny Bug with, at best, 50bhp. Not for the VW owner the experience of mashing the throttle and seeing the tyres go up in smoke. Driving a stock VW in the 1950s and early '60s was a more leisurely experience. Soon, however, all that was to change…

The European Volkswagen aftermarket industry was in the ascendancy, and many of the products were now being exported across the

Atlantic for consumption by VW enthusiasts in the USA. And, thanks to the National Hot Rod Association's desire to accommodate every type of vehicle in one class or another, the Beetle had the opportunity to shine.

The earliest reference the author has come across of a Volkswagen taking to the drag strip was a report (and accompanying photograph) of a stock Oval-window Beetle on the start line of a long-lost track as far back as 1954. The caption reported that the VW was "easily beaten" by the British-built Singer Roadster shown in the other lane. But once the Beetle fell into the hands of people like Dean Lowry, the tables would begin to turn. Lowry cut his teeth on Volkswagens while working at Joe Vittone's Economotors VW dealership in Riverside, California. He joined the company in 1955, serving as a mechanic, and soon came to appreciate the sound engineering (and ease of maintenance) which would come to endear the VW to generations of enthusiasts.

Lowry left Economotors after a few years and went to work for Century Motors in Alhambra. There, his inherent love of drag racing led him to prepare a Beetle for use at the nearby San Gabriel drag strip. Running in handicap events, or simply just for time-slips, Lowry attracted the attention of the local Volkswagen representatives, who told him that they could not sanction his use of the company name on a "competition vehicle". Instead, Lowry built a Porsche-engined dragster and drove that, much to the delight of the local Porsche sales team.

When Vittone asked Lowry to join his Economotors-based European Motor Products, Inc (EMPI) business in 1963, he seized the opportunity because it offered him the chance to work on developing a range of performance products for the Beetle – and to help prepare what would become the company's race car, a 1956 VW sedan, owned by Vittone senior's son, Darrell. Used as his daily driver to and from college, the red Oval-window Beetle sported a set of chrome wheels and a home-brewed sports muffler on the otherwise stock 36hp motor. The car would go on to become arguably the most famous VW race car in history, *Inch Pincher*, seeing action on both the drag strip and the race circuit, the latter exploits in the hands of Dan Gurney at the Nassau Grand Prix of Volkswagens in 1962 and 1963.

For the most part, performance-enhancing products of the time were of varied quality, but certain names, such as Okrasa and Denzel, stood head and shoulders above the rest, with their well-engineered cylinder heads, forged crankshafts and, in the case of the Denzel conversion, beautifully-crafted aluminium conrods. Dual carburettors, sourced from the Porsche parts catalogue, added the finishing touch, helping to boost the output of the basic 30bhp (36hp SAE) engine by more than 50 per cent. On the west coast of America, these conversions were available through EMPI in Riverside, helping to prove to Californian enthusiasts that there could, indeed, be the heart of a lion beating within the humble Bug.

But scan the pages of magazines of the era – most notable among them *Foreign Car Guide*, published in Ohio by Rajo Publications, Inc – and you cannot cease to be amazed by the sheer volume of advertisements for what purported to be performance products for the Volkswagen. For example, Fisher Products of New York and Culver City, California, imported four-pipe Abarth mufflers from Italy, while the Judson Research & Manufacturing Co of Conshohocken, Pennsylvania, marketed its own vane-design supercharger. The latter was a very popular conversion in the 1950s, being a simple bolt-on kit that gave almost Okrasa-like performance, yet requiring modest mechanical skills to fit it.

Some companies fought shy of actually telling the reader what was included in the conversion. Lion Products from Denver, Colorado, offered the Lion GT kit, with its "three steps to more power, safely – saves gas, too". One can only hazard a guess at what the GT kit might have consisted of but, for the most part, these little-known conversions comprised little more than an extra stock carburettor, a pair of manifolds and a crude throttle linkage. They could be bolted on in a weekend and promised greatly enhanced performance – a promise that was rarely delivered in full.

What most of these companies had come to realise was that, in stock form, the Volkswagen engine was being deliberately strangled by the induction system. VW had never intended the Beetle to be a performance car, leaving such matters to its sibling, Porsche. The combination of a diminutive single-throat carburettor, long, restrictive manifold and tiny inlet valves meant that the engine's breathing capacity was severely restricted – and for good reason. Essentially, the Beetle was intended to last for ever, cruising the Autobahns at a steady 100km/h

(62mph) in relative comfort.

So just what was theoretically available on the open market to help boost the performance of a budding hot-rodder's VW? In Dick Morgan's book, *Souping the Volkswagen*, published by Floyd Clymer in 1959, unsurprisingly there are numerous references to both the Okrasa and Denzel conversions. Car Tecnik in Washington was listed as the importer of the well-received German "Express" carburettor kit, while O W Dietz Engineering Co of Detroit, Michigan, offered its own dual carburettor kit. For just $48.00, the customer would receive polished dual-intake manifolds, "sturdy" throttle linkage, choke connection (to one carburettor only), fuel lines with adaptor, heat riser cover plates and an instruction manual. In addition, the purchaser would need to buy a second Solex carburettor for $33.00, making a grand total of $81.00 for a claimed increase in power of 18 per cent. The similar Express conversion was more expensive, at $117, but for that the customer was promised a 25 per cent boost in output.

To take things a stage

*Carlsbad Raceway was nicknamed "Carlsdirt" for good reason! Lowry's **Dyno-Soar** waits in line. (Jim Edmiston)*

*Published in 1959, **Souping the Volkswagen** was among the first books on the subject. (Author's collection)*

Earl McMills of Inglewood, California, was the man to whom many turned to buy speed equipment in the early 1960s. (Ron Fleming)

Ken Ullyett's 1962 **The Porsche and Volkswagen Companion** *was a high-quality hardback edition. (Author's collection)*

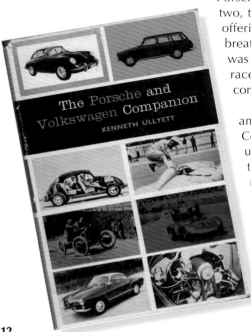

further would mean pulling the engine out and splitting the crankcase – that way you could change the camshaft or, if your finances would allow it, swap the stock crank for a "stroker". In 1960, the big names in camshaft technology were Iskendarian (Isky), Howard Racing Cams, Harman-Collins and Weber (not to be confused with the Italian company Weber, which made carburettors). These companies would take a stock camshaft and regrind the lobes to give more lift and duration. Hot choices for fast road cars were the Iskendarian 2B and 2J grinds, based on the profile of the cam used in the Porsche Super 90 engine. Of the two, the 2J was the more radical, offering greater lift for better breathing. An Iskendarian 103A was also available, being a "full-race" camshaft designed for competition use.

To go with these cams, Isky and the Beck Distributing Company could supply uprated valve springs, while the former also sold chrome-moly valve spring retainers for high-rpm use. Of course, back then, high-rpm meant little more than 5500rpm – a far cry from the 8000-plus rpm seen by today's hot VWs.

Long-stroke cranks were available from Okrasa and imported into the USA by EMPI. They were high-quality, if expensive, forgings which increased the capacity from 1192cc to 1286cc. Cheaper alternatives were the domestically produced crankshafts from Weber Tool Co. Available as either quarter-inch or half-inch strokers (giving approximately a 6mm and 12mm increase over the stock stroke, respectively), the Weber cranks were machined from solid billets of cast steel and came as part of complete kits, including stroker pistons, balanced con-rods and piston rings. The quarter-inch kit raised the capacity to 1310cc and cost $199.50 (with exchange rods), while the half-inch kit took the capacity up to 1427cc and cost $237.50 – but that price included a reground camshaft, too.

There were no commercially-available big-bore cylinder kits at the turn of the decade, but it was possible to bore the stock cylinders out by as much as 2mm, giving a five per cent increase in engine capacity. Replacement Hepolite pistons were available in long-stroke conversions. The most exotic option was to use the aluminium cylinders offered by Porsche but, at some $250 a set, they were deemed to be too costly by most people.

Even by the early- to mid-sixties there were relatively few places where you could buy performance parts at an affordable price. EMPI could supply piston and cylinder kits to turn an 1192cc engine into a 1340cc "big-bore" conversion (using machined-down cylinders from a 1500cc engine), along with a growing range of dress-up parts, or sell you a pair of Stromberg carburettors on Speedwell manifolds. Ron Fleming, now of FAT Performance in Orange, CA, recalls that most people went to see "an old guy by the name of Earl McMills", a retired machinist from one of the aircraft companies. He was located in Inglewood, CA. "You went through his garage to a shop built on the back and that is where he cast cylinders and who knows what else." This near-legendary figure would produce, as if by magic, such parts as long-stoke cranks, reground cams and other pieces vital to building a quick VW at a time when such components were rarely available elsewhere.

Jim Edmiston – one of the founding fathers of the original Der Kleiner Panzers Volkswagen Club – the seminal club located in Orange County, California – recalls McMills, too: "All of us have heard of Dean Lowry, Berg and Vittone, but what about Earl McMills? The very first

Crudely-drawn handout was placed under the windshield wipers of prospective candidates for membership of Der Kleiner Panzers. From little acorns did mighty oak trees grow… (Greg Bunch)

stroker crank club member Mike Mahaffey bought was a welded piece that lasted only a few runs before giving up. Ron Fleming knew of Earl… that he had 'stuff' in his small garage to make VWs haul ass. So, Ron and Mike paid him a visit, and Mike left with an 82mm SPG stroker crank and, in later trips, dual-port heads and even a limited-slip differential. I made the trip

once and bought an intake manifold for my newly-acquired Zenith 32NDIX carburettor."

When Volkswagen introduced the 1500 engine in the Transporter range in January 1963, suddenly the Beetle's stock 1192cc, 34bhp ("40-horse") motor seemed positively underpowered. The new, larger engine immediately provided a long-stroke (69mm instead of 66mm) crankshaft and more efficient cylinder heads, but at a cost which was, initially at least, prohibitive to many on a tight budget. Gradually, though, such motors became available from junkyards and many found their way into Bugs – or at least,

With tracks like Carlsbad, Lions, Irwindale and OCIR all close at hand, there was never any shortage of opportunity for club members to check out their cars' potential. Note the Porsche rims, traction bar and long "stinger" exhaust. (Ron Fleming)

Rare photograph of DKP member Don Crane's brand-new 1967 sedan. Check the Goodyear Blue Streak tyres, raised front end (for superior weight transfer) and blue-tinted Plexiglass side windows. (Jim Holmes)

13

American Racing five-spoke wheels were Fleming's trademark. (Ron Fleming)

*Schley Brothers' first **Lightning Bug** was ultimately destroyed in a horrific roll-over accident at Orange County International Raceway. (Jim Edmiston)*

Taking photographs of your car in an unusual setting seemed to be a popular pastime back in the 1960s! Ron Fleming's Oval-window sedan looks slightly out of place under the trees... (Ron Fleming)

were used as parts donors for high-performance rebuilds.

Jim Edmiston, recalls his first efforts at building his own "hot" VW: "It was around 1969 when I bought a used 1500cc engine (it was guaranteed to run, of course...) from a 'core' (junk) guy that fellow club member Ron Fleming knew. I can't tell you how excited I was to get started. My goal was to build a 1600 engine (using the cylinders from a later Type 2) with an Engle 110 cam, single-port heads (machined for more compression, but who really knew how much more?), a Zenith 32NDIX carburettor and an S&S competition exhaust. I'd had plenty of experience watching others build VW engines, so why shouldn't I give it a try?

"Rule number one: never force anything – including cylinders that needed a little 'help'

Hank Elfrink's **Making Your Volkswagen Go!** *was published in 1960 and is regarded as one of the most informative books of its time. (Author's collection)*

with a piece of wood and a mallet. Unfortunately, I chose a ball-peen hammer, instead, resulting in a large compression leak on all four cylinders. Rule number two: they put those arrows on top of the pistons for a reason. Rule number three: there really are five main-bearing dowel pins, not four. You get the idea… But, let's face it, you'll never learn unless you try. It's just too bad learning has to be so hard sometimes!"

For Edmiston (known to all and sundry as "Sarge" for reasons we'll explain later), the early days of the VW scene were times of camaraderie, partying – and, to use the official expression, exhibitions of speed. The VW scene in Southern California was a fairly tight-knit community, with a growing number of enthusiasts each turning to the same parts suppliers for help and assistance. Unlike today – when it is possible to pick up a telephone and order virtually everything to build a high-horsepower motor from scratch, using nothing more than an on-line catalogue and a credit card – in the 1960s your options were severely limited.

Early modified Beetles tended to adopt a fairly clear-cut style, one typified by Darrell Vittone's Oval-window Bug referred to earlier. The style of Vittone's car at this time was an amalgam of customising methods employed by just about every impecunious young enthusiast across America, rather than being a conscious attempt to set any new trend within the VW scene. While alloy wheels – popularly referred to as "mags" in deference to the high magnesium content which many castings enjoyed – were available in the late 1950s and early 1960s, they

Chromed Porsche 356 rims with nipple hubcaps were a popular choice in the late 1960s. (Ken Jevec)

Dave Pekor's sedan featured reversed-offset rims on the rear, with Bluestreak tyres, Porsche front wheels and a cool racing stripe. (Ken Jevec)

Roy Jiminez was among the first to race a 'late-model' sedan. Check the crudely flared rear fenders and the use of 13-inch rims, with oval-track slick tyres. (Jim Holmes)

Sporting offset Porsche rims and devoid of any style of bumper, Greg Aronson's rag-top sedan displays its new Don Bradford interior. (Jim Holmes)

*Fully-dressed Okrasa engine was the height of cool when this **Hot Rod Magazine** special edition was published in 1963. (Author's collection)*

dangerous!) as the bolts no longer seated correctly on the wheel.

One thing that's easy to forget is that so many of the cars which were modified back in the early- to mid-1960s were rarely more than five years old – and many of them much younger than that. In fact, it was not at all uncommon for a brand-new Beetle, bought maybe as a graduation present, to be turned into a VW enthusiast's idea of a hot-rod within weeks or even days of ownership.

One such person was DKP founder member John Lazenby, who bought a brand-new Beetle in July 1963 from Joe Vittone's Economotors in Riverside. It didn't remain stock for long, as Lazenby clearly recalls: "In 1964 I purchased my first set of chrome wheels (they were VW 'solids', rather than those from a Porsche 356). Later that same year I installed the first set of Four-tuned 'fresh-air' headers ever made." Bob Sanchez, John Lazenby and Joe Schneider, who owned Schneider Motors, the dealership which sponsored the club, fitted the new exhaust system. "I learned some Spanish and German that day, I can tell you! I had 'Fourtuned Headers' painted on the rear fenders and my parents were not pleased at all…". The next step was to fit a Judson supercharger and head for the nearby Lions Drag Strip. "Unfortunately, the Judson cooked number three piston in short fashion, and so a set of 83mm big-bore cylinders

Engine-turned inserts placed in the headlamp bowls was a simple yet eye-catching trick favoured by many enthusiasts in the 1960s. (Jim Edmiston)

were expensive and generally only suited for use on larger domestic vehicles, rather than the little Volkswagen, due to their width and offset.

Less expensive chromed steel wheels were, however, widely available – even for the Volkswagen, with its unique "wide-five" wheel bolt pattern. They were a godsend for young car nuts, whose budgets rarely stretched much further than a cheap set of wheels and a loud exhaust. Factory-made (or cheaper aftermarket) rims designed for use on a Porsche 356 could be bolted straight on to a Beetle without the need for adaptors, and gave Vittone and others like him the opportunity to mount wider tyres for better handling.

Also popular was the process of grafting the centre section of a stock Volkswagen wheel into the wider rim of a domestic vehicle, thereby gaining extra width but not at the expense of an incompatible offset – which could cause clearance problems between the tyre and bodywork, or place the tyre too far outside the fender. There was also a trend for simply turning the stock VW wheels round and bolting them onto the hubs, back-to-front… This resulted in a "wide-track" look favoured by some, but was not a recommended conversion (for that read: highly

was installed. I ran that set-up for a number of years," says Lazenby.

The year 1965 also saw the car get repainted Firemist Green, a 1964 or '65 Cadillac Eldorado colour. Lazenby remembers he then installed a set of wide glassfibre fenders on the rear to cover the American Racing Torq-Thrust mags (in Chevrolet bolt pattern) and Firestone Indy-type tyres. "Prior to installing those fenders, the tyres hung out too far, so I cut and fitted aluminium strips that ran round most of the fender to cover the tread.

"In 1967, I went on active duty in the US Navy, and the car was stored at my parents' house until I returned in April 1969. Shortly thereafter I became active in DKP once more, but lots had changed since I left." As Ron Fleming recalls, the club had become more performance-oriented, and the style of club cars began to change. Lazenby swapped the wide American Racing wheels for some narrower Porsche chrome rims. The front suspension was lowered, the bumpers removed and Ron Fleming built a 1700cc

motor with a Holley Bugspray carburettor, Engle 110 camshaft and a set of S&S exhaust headers. Within a short time Lazenby broke the gearbox, so he took the opportunity to install a set of close-ratio gears. The car ran

Art Alvarez's fully-dechromed 1967 Bug ran a set of unusual Mag Climax wheels, which featured steel rims on cast aluminium centres. (Art Alvarez)

La Palma Park in Anaheim was the setting for this early get together of Der Kleiner Panzer club members. Notice how many of the cars are almost stock in appearance. (Ron Fleming)

Racing at Carlsbad often continued into the late evening. Dirt entry road (right) was a dust-storm waiting to happen... (Ron Fleming)

One-off mufflers, like that on Mike Johnston's Bug (far right), were popular in the 1960s. (Mike Johnston)

Early photograph of the first Underdog race car being flat-towed to Carlsbad Raceway for a test session. (Ron Fleming)

low 15-second quarter-miles in that form.

The last major change Lazenby made to the car was in 1971, when he went to Leonard Becker's paint shop for a respray in a Chevrolet hue: Warbonnet Yellow. At the same time, he had Becker weld up all the holes left following the removal of the hood- and side-trim, along with the bumper holes and the two exhaust cut-outs in the rear apron. Don Bradford was called in to retrim the interior in a theme inspired by the stretched "Limo Bug" owned by Volkswagen of America that was around at that time. "I wanted something more than a sparse race-style interior and I didn't want black," says Lazenby. "In the end, we chose to do it in a dark brown, with seat inserts that looked like suede. The carpet and headliner were dark brown, with the

headliner being the same suede-like material as the seat inserts. Brad also made a dark brown sun-roof covering, and even a 'bra' for the car to match. The trunk was all custom and had a really cool toolbox.

"There were two panels made for the dashboard, both of which were covered with the suede material and edged with the brown vinyl.

Ron Fleming ran a Zenith two-barrel carburettor on a custom manifold. Three-bolt exhaust header hooked up to a chromed glass-pack. (Ron Fleming)

The glovebox door was done the same to match. The original gauges were replaced by a set of the old VDO yellow-faced instruments. I also found a Butler wood-rimmed wheel that looked very much like a Nardi, but the Butler's horn button was nicer, or so I thought. I also fitted a DDS gear shifter. By this time, the cops were coming down on all VWs with lowered front ends, so I installed air-shocks up front with a pump and the control in the glove box." When the cops saw Lazenby's lowered Beetle drive past, they would invariably do a quick U-turn and go after him. "By that time, I'd hit the button and backed off the gas. The vacuum raised the car, so when the cops pulled me over they would look puzzled as to why the car was no longer low!"

As part of this major revision of his car, John Lazenby decided it was time to step up the performance. "Somewhere along this last trip, I built the 78.4mm x 88mm (1900cc) motor with 48IDA Weber carburettors mounted on tall EMPI manifolds. I can't precisely remember the cam, but it was maybe an Engle FK89 with high-ratio rocker arms. Ron (Fleming) did the heads and I used an S&S header with merged collector. But, after driving it like this, I became tired of the noise and decided to install Berg manifolds with a pair of his 42DCNF Webers. At the same time, I took out the close-ratio gears and put heater boxes back on. I really liked the car much better this way, as it was still fast and I could go anywhere."

Mike Mahaffey's impressive collection of memorabilia includes early DKP newsletters, dinner invitations (how stylish is that!) and several designs of club membership cards. The Panzers were probably the most organised of clubs in the early days. (Mike Mahaffey)

The biggest thrill, recalls Ron Fleming, was cruising down the Freeway with fellow club members. Traffic would literally come a halt to watch the line of VWs head on by. (Ron Fleming)

One of the trademark features of John Lazenby's car, aside from the Warbonnet Yellow paint, which led to the car being referred to as "Butternut" by all and sundry, was the choice of wheels – magnesium American Torq-Thrusts. "I almost forgot the Americans. The first pair came from a girl driving a Baja Bug. I spotted them on her car, chased her down the road and bought them for just $40. Then Doug Haydon found the inventory of Americans from the warehouse and between us we bought them all. From those came my (five) new ones. I guess I sold the used

Drinking beer down Mexico way... Trips south of the border were a popular way to have fun for many DKP members. The age of innocence would soon come to an end with the draft and the possibility of service in Vietnam. (Ron Fleming)

ones, but honestly don't remember now. We didn't like the fake knock-off centre-caps, so I went to American and found the hex-design caps, which I ended up using. Later, I painted the spokes a dark brown to match the sunroof and interior. Chas Sihilling, in Santa Ana, did the polished rims – and he still does my work today.

"I sold the car in October or November of '74 as I recall. At the time I could only get about $1600 for it complete with the Americans, 1900cc Okrasa motor, 42DCNF Webers – everything. It makes me sick when I think about it now. Within months of me selling the car it was rolled and destroyed. Somewhere along the way Don Chamberlin got the wheels, but I don't know where any of the rest of it ended up.

"The car was sold because my wife Christie and I had just purchased our first home and our life was changing. Also I'd become interested in buying a BMW, which I did. But lifelong friendships and love formed while I had that car – and those are things you simply can't replace."

If there's one sentiment that comes through strong and clear whenever any club member talks of these early days of the California Look, it's that the camaraderie was second to none. It was as if they were all pioneers of a new age. Which, of course, is precisely what they were…

The show card for John Lazenby's car reads like a who's-who of the VW scene in the late 1960s and early 1970s: engine by Fleming and Aronson, paint by Leonard Becker and an interior by Don "Brad" Bradford. Things don't get much better than that…
(Jim Edmiston)

Without doubt one of the most stylish of all early DKP cars was John Lazenby's "Butternut" sedan. With its distinctive GM Warbonnet Yellow paint and magnesium Torq-Thrust wheels, it was a real head-turner.
(Ron Fleming)

Chapter 2

ACTING CRAZY AND HAVING FUN

"That's where the cops showed up and ushered us back over to the Pickwick. Sometimes, I wonder how we all made it!"
Jim Edmiston

1960s

Jim Edmiston was one of the founder members of Der Kleiner Panzers – and was right there at the start of the whole So Cal VW speed scene. He's lived and breathed Volkswagens since his teenage years and has a memory that's second to none. In so many ways, his story is typical of any young VW enthusiast growing up in Orange County in the 1960s, yet what makes his tale almost unique is the fact that his enthusiasm for, and personal involvement with, VWs has remained undiminished for over 40 years.

Jim and Sharon Edmiston wax their 1956 Oval-window Beetle outside Jim's parents' house – note his dad's 1963 sedan in the background. At this point the Oval was stock other than repainted wheels and brake drums. (Jim Edmiston)

"My first car was a 1956 Oval-window sedan, which I bought for 300 bucks back in 1964. My dad already had a similar car, which I liked, so I decided I had to have one. Of course, me being a kid in California, I couldn't leave things alone. I just had to mess with it!" recalls Edmiston.

"Back then, there weren't too many parts to buy for VWs, and about all you could get was a velocity stack for the carburettor, a Bosch 'Blue' six-volt coil and a pair of straight-through tailpipes to make some noise. The Oval-window was fun, but I knew I wanted something a little more up to date, so it had to go…

"My second car was a 1963 sedan that my parents had purchased new from Lee Wood Motors in Whittier, CA. I eventually bought it off them around 1965, after I sold the '56. I had to have the '63 because it was a newer model!"

Back in the 1960s, during what is known as the "Pre-Cal Look" era, changes to a car's appearance were relatively few and far between. "Cosmetically, we didn't do much to the cars back then," says Jim, "besides painting the

Among the first changes made by Edmiston to his parents' 1963 Beetle was to fit American five-spoke rims to the front, and Ansen slot-mags to the rear (far left). The front wheels were later changed to narrowed Porsche rims (left), while the Ansens were painted black. Note the Four-Tuned exhaust system. (Jim Edmiston)

wheels and the drums, installing an extractor exhaust system and fitting Plexiglas quarter windows – mine were tinted yellow. Inside, we'd mount a Cobico three-spoke steering wheel, but only a few people in the club could afford extra instruments.

"In 1967, the car was passed on to my wife-to-be, Sharon, when I got drafted into the US Army and headed off on a tour of duty in Vietnam. Up to that point, any modifications made had been fairly minimal, at least by today's standards. There was a Four-Tuned exhaust, 010 distributor and that velocity stack. Like many club members, I planned to swap the wheels and use adaptors to install rims with the Chevy bolt pattern. I eventually had American Racing wheels on the front and Ansen Sprints on the back. Sharon made these changes while I was visiting Vietnam.

"Upon returning stateside in 1969, I found that the club's main focus had shifted to more serious performance. The mag wheels and adaptors had given way to lighter chrome wheels so, at this point, I ran Porsche 356 rims at the front, narrowed to 3.5 inches and equipped with skinny little 125 tyres from a Citroën." Clearly, wet-weather handling wasn't the Bug's strong point, not that this was much of a concern in southern California!

Edmiston continues: "We also used to pull torsion leaves from the front axle beam to give our cars a nose-down stance, like the race cars of the day. Some of the guys also dechromed their cars – but not everybody did. My focus throughout this process was always on ways to make my car as fast as possible while spending the least amount of money."

Club cars were under constant development, with the honour of appearing on the DKP "Top Ten" list being a prime motivator for many members. Edmiston remembers his attempts at making his mark: "Back in those days, I had an 1835cc motor in my '63, with 0.0120 inches fly-cut out of the Ron Fleming ported and polished 40mmx35.5mm heads, an Engle 125 camshaft (which had been retarded by 4 degrees), Weber 48IDA carburettors and a gearbox with a 4.37:1 final drive and close-ratio gears. I raced the snot out of this car for a good year, running 13.20s at 95–97mph on radial tyres. The thing pulled like a bear in third gear, probably as a result of the retarded cam timing. I used NPR cast pistons – and the ring grooves wore quickly if you ran lots of compression. That was a common problem."

If you read magazine features of the time, it's easy to believe that all Cal Lookers from the late 1960s and early 1970s benefited from the magic

A proud Jim Edmiston poses at the wheel of his Oval-window. The large decal in the rear quarter window boasted "Genuine Volkswagen Parts" – but as yet there was no DKP affiliation. (Jim Edmiston)

American Racing wheels featured a Chevrolet bolt-pattern and were fitted using adaptors, which pushed the tyres outside the fenders. (Jim Edmiston)

Chromed Porsche rims eventually replaced the US-made mags. (Jim Edmiston)

fibre bucket seats from Auto Haus – which were mounted to stripped VW seat frames (I splurged here and had mine chromed), aluminium door panels and removing as much inner door bracing as possible. The rear seat backrest was quickly discarded, as well as the heater ducting under the back seat cushion."

The highlight of Jim's dashboard was an aluminium plate used to cover the radio opening: "I added some toggle switches and idiot lights for the 'race look'. Needless to say, with a close-ratio gearbox and solid transmission mounts, you couldn't hear yourself think after a few minutes behind the wheel! When I look back on all this, I find it amazing to think that the car was only six years old when all that went on. In real terms, it was still a nearly-new car!"

Back when Der Kleiner Panzers first started, Edmiston spent most of his time hanging out with fellow club member John Lazenby, who worked at Auto Haus, the chain of VW parts stores in Orange County, CA. To begin with, club meetings were held at various members' homes. "John and I would spend our Saturdays waxing our cars at his folk's place in Anaheim. That's how the paint on my '63 literally wore out!" laughs Edmiston. "In those days, the wax of choice was Classic. Brian Renie (who owned a black '65 sedan – it was the cleanest of them all!) always had a dozen empty Classic wax cans stacked neatly in the garage; the guy was totally anal about waxing his car.

touch of skilled trimmers such as Don "Brad" Bradford. But reality was far different. Jim Edmiston remembers that: "The interior in my '63 sedan could best be described as 'spartan'. I simply never had the money to pay for a nice interior, as what little cash I had always found its way into the engine compartment!

"In keeping with my desire to go as fast as possible, for little money and with small engine combos, shaving weight off the car seemed the logical way to proceed. That meant stripping all the tar board from the floor, fitting a pair of glass-

Sharon Edmiston has shared husband Jim's passion for VWs since the very beginning. Note the presence of the DKP club decal in this photo. (Jim Edmiston)

"After all the detailing at John's house, we'd go get our gals and head over to Carl's Jr (the original one on Harbor and Romneya) and have dinner. Then it was time to go cruising with the Muntz four-track tape blasting away. We'd listen to The Who, Led Zeppelin and, later, Hendrix – all the good rock stuff. A lot of times, we'd just drive around in a loop between Carl's, Taco Villa, Hillcrest Park and The Bean Hut. Other times we'd drive up to Hollywood and loop down Hollywood Boulevard and Sunset, stopping at Tiny Naylor's for a Cherry Vanilla Coke. Back then, there was little in the way of traffic, so those drives were cheap, easy entertainment.

"Another place we used to cruise to was Harvey's Charbroiler, with a stop at Wenzel's Music Town for a stack of 45rpm records to throw in John's car-mounted ARC record changer. These places always had lots of V8s sitting outside, whether muscle cars, hot rods, or something new right off the showroom floor. VWs were always the butt of the joke, so to speak… so you can see right where this was headed: V8, whoop ass! It seems that things were a lot easier back then…"

Driving their cars was a big part of the club scene in the late 1960s. "Back then, you could actually cruise around Orange County – and one of my favourite drives was Laguna Canyon Road. You could begin or end a trip to the beach on a nice, gently curving country road. My wife and I spent many weekends cruising up and down Pacific Coast Highway in a VW. It was a fun drive, with beautiful scenery thrown in. Nowadays, it's pretty much gridlocked. Memories…"

Partying, though, was a big deal. And party the club members did, as Edmiston recalls with glee: "These parties always started at the clubhouse and revolved around a game of what we called 'Thumper' to get things going. To the uninitiated, Thumper is a game played sitting on the floor (which is a good thing) in a circle with your drink of choice. The game begins with one guy chanting: 'What's the name of the game?', at which the other players holler 'THUMPER!'. 'How do you play?' 'Make a SIGN!' – everyone playing had their own sign, such as a thumb on the forehead, thumb down, two fingers up, etc.

"The person starting the game then flashed his sign and the sign of another player, who must then flash his own sign and someone else's, and so-on until there was a screw-up. The guy who screwed up had to drain his drink, and the whole deal started over again. Needless to say,

things got ugly real fast!

"After everyone was 'loosened up"', we would do crazy stuff, such as take a visit to the Garden Theater for a 'nice movie' (we're talking adult entertainment here, folks, in downtown Anaheim). Greg Aronson and his brother Jeff were in the front row when Greg had to hurl – Jeff quickly pulled off one of shoes and passed Greg a sock to use as a barf bag. Needless to say, we all got escorted out after that!

"Another time we had a train of 15–20 guys doing the Samba down Anaheim Blvd, through

Swapping mufflers was a common trick – some photos of Jim's car show the glasspack exiting to the left side, as above.
(Jim Edmiston)

Back from the military, "Sarge" Edmiston got to enjoy his Bug – or was it Sharon's? – once more.
(Jim Edmiston)

The '63's dashboard took on many forms. Note here the tacho mounted in the speaker panel on the left and the rally plaques on the glovebox door. (Jim Edmiston)

Relocated tacho, switch panel in place of radio, new shifter – Jim's car was constantly evolving. Chrome dash panels remained, though. (Jim Edmiston)

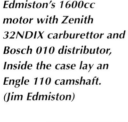

Engine shown is Edmiston's 1600cc motor with Zenith 32NDIX carburettor and Bosch 010 distributor. Inside the case lay an Engle 110 camshaft. (Jim Edmiston)

Elmer's Play-More Lounge (the watering hole across from the clubhouse at the Pickwick Hotel), over to Don's (adult) book store (it was really quiet in there – or not! I think owner Don called the cops, too) and back diagonally through the intersection of Anaheim Blvd and Lincoln Ave. That's where the cops showed up and ushered us back over to the Pickwick. Sometimes, I wonder how we all made it!"

Despite this carefree outlook, these were uncertain times for returning soldiers like Edmiston – or "Sarge" as he was now known, in deference to his military rank. "When I got out of the Army, I had no idea what I wanted to do for a living. Back then it was customary for returning servicemen to have their Army life insurance 'converted' to a civilian insurance company. After lying around doing nothing for a couple of weeks, I got booted out of the house and was forced to get some kind of job! That's when an insurance agent came by and, after converting my insurance, recruited me into the insurance business. Well, I did pretty well for a while, then I got lazy. I only had to report to the office on Tuesdays and Fridays, which left three days for 'visiting' my friends at their jobs or hanging out at the beach.

"My time was split between going to BAP Geon (to see club members Stan Davis, Doug and Whit Haydon, and Dan Czapla), Snow's Foreign Car (Roy Jimenez), Gene Berg Enterprises (on Lemon St, in Orange, to call by Greg Aronson and Ron Fleming), or Greg Aronson's house after he'd left Berg's, and then, later on, Ron and Greg at Fleming & Aronson. Luckily for me, my wife had a real job!

A youthful "Sarge" shows off a captured AK47 while on service in Vietnam. (Jim Edmiston)

"Greg Aronson did quite well working out of his parents' garage back then. I'd help with pulling motors and transmissions out of cars, then we'd pile in 'The Toilet' (the nickname for Aronson's white bus, with its trademark bungee cord round the shifter to hold it in fourth gear) and head off to Engine Dynamics (balancing), National Crank (crank grinders), Ollie's Automotive (machine work), BAP Geon (parts), and so on. Then we'd head back to the house, where Greg's dad had a beer tap in the den for a little refreshment. Unfortunately, all good things eventually come to an end (especially when the money runs out) and I was forced to find a real job for myself."

Sarge ran a variety of engine combinations, including a 1600cc motor with an Engle 110 cam, Bosch 010 distributor and a Zenith 32NDIX carb, which he felt was a good set-up. Next, he stepped up to 1700cc, with 11:1 compression heads ported by Ron Fleming at FAT – and then the close-ratio gearbox came along. He ran a Holley 300cfm Bugspray carb for a short time, as well as dual Solex 40P11s. The Weber 48IDAs followed soon after, probably around 1970–71. "For a while, I also used a 74x88mm engine, which translated to 1800cc – I bought it from Greg Aronson," recalls Sarge, "but I quickly busted the crankshaft! The biggest engine I ultimately installed was an 1835cc with 48IDAs. We raced at Lions Drag Strip – until it closed in 1972 – and at Orange County Raceway on Wednesday nights."

Participating at the legendary OCIR Bug-Ins was an important part of the lives of VW enthusiasts in southern California. Der Kleiner Panzers also held a number of Drag Days at Carlsbad Raceway, as well as rallies, which attracted as many as 200 partcipants in the years between 1969 and '71. They street raced among themselves – and with other car clubs, and V8s, too. It seems that every weekend something was going on, until the club's activities eventually drew to a close in 1972.

Street racing played a big part in the lives of young enthusiasts back in the late '60s and early 1970s. Somehow, it seemed less stigmatised than it does today, but was probably just as dangerous. There were several favourite 'venues' at which the settling of scores would take place, among them behind the Nabisco factory, Pacific Stereo or on La Palma Avenue, all in Orange County, California.

"My memory of racing at Nabisco involved

Jim raced his car regularly at the drags – it eventually ran low-thirteens. He also helped Ron Fleming and Doug Gordon with the Underdog (above left). (Jim Edmiston)

The '63 ultimately ran an 1835cc engine with dual 48IDA carburettors on short manifolds, hooked up to a close-ratio transmission. Note the Berg carb linkage. (Jim Edmiston)

In 1969, using money he received on leaving the Army, Edmiston bought a brand new Beetle to run alongside his Datsun pick-up truck. (JIm Edmiston)

The car was driven everywhere and in every kind of weather. Lowered front suspension and chromed wheels were soon added. (Jim Edmiston)

going against my neighbour's Dodge Super Bee in my '63 sedan, with its 1835cc IDA motor and short gears. We raced for $20, which was a lot of money way back then!" laughs Sarge. "I lost by a fender-length, but I was with Ron Fleming at the time, who came along with Doug and Whit Haydon. The Haydons set up another race for double or nothing between my neighbour and Whit Haydon's car, which was across town in their garage. We all caravanned over to the Haydons' shop on Fender St – but what my neighbour failed to realize was how fast and how much more horsepower Whit's car had. As far as he was concerned, it was simply another VW to squash.

"When Whit backed his car out of the shop with a stinger on the exhaust, my neighbour wouldn't race until he uncorked his headers, too. Well, you guessed it – Whit smoked the guy bad! Then we all had to bail quick into the Haydons' shop to avoid the cops, who showed up almost immediately. Both those guys had nice, fast cars. Doug owned a 1967 sedan in Lotus white, which was later painted what we referred to as 'Vick's Bottle Blue', with five-spoke American Racing rims (from John Lazenby), while Whit raced a Sepia Brown '56 sedan. When it came time to race, those two cats were always the first to jump – and if they lost, they knew how to fight!"

In 1972, after "screwing around at my insurance job", Sarge took his first real job at a VW dealership, Renfree Motors, as a parts technician. "I figured that, since I was in a VW club, it would be no problem selling VW parts. Well, I started my day at the mechanic's counter with a Frenchman named Pierre, who had a Type 3 automatic trans in a million pieces. I soon discovered I knew absolutely nothing – and neither did Pierre. I lasted about eight months before bailing out," recalls Edmiston. That prompted a move to Sierra Porsche Audi, at Riverside, CA.

Sarge continues: "Compared to my short stint at Renfree VW, working with Harvey Weidman at Sierra Porsche Audi was quite an experience. I'd known Harvey from high school days, and his older brother, Al, had taught me to swim many years before. Before Harvey became Parts Manager at Sierra, he had spent a number of years working at Paint by Molly in La Habra (Molly was responsible for the paint on Vittone's *Inch Pincher Too* gasser).

"The Porsche parts business was strong back in the mid-1970s and, along with all the normal stuff we used to sell, Harvey got involved with buying direct from Stuttgart. We imported hundreds of Fuchs alloys back then, and loads of Turbo and Carrera weld-on flares, too. When Darrell Vittone, who ran the dyno at Economotors/Race Shop at the time, was building his 1972 911S, we got him some factory Recaro seats, along with a limited-slip differential, low-ratio ring and pinion and a set of short 'airport' gears. It was a four-mile drive to Economotors, and we had many lunchtime cruises together in either my Datsun pick-up, Darrell's '56 bug, or the 911. Sometimes we'd be joined by Darrell's friend Carl 'Grub' Robinson. Grub and I soon

While working with Harvey Weidman, Edmiston decided to "Porsche-ize" his '69, with blacked-out trim and Mahle wheels from a Porsche 914. "Bra" protected paintwork from stone chips. (Jim Edmiston)

became best of friends – my wife and I spent a lot of our weekends hanging out at his compound in Highgrove (which was aptly named the Highgrove Gypsy Camp). Grub's beautiful camo-painted Ghia took us on many orange grove tours back in the day.

"For helping Darrell with parts for his 911, I was given an engine for my Datsun truck that had been built for a customer's Datsun 510 track car, but was never picked up and had been around The Race Shop for a year or two. Fumio (Fukaya) did the head and it had a Racer Brown cam, 2000 Roadster clutch and flywheel, dual Solex-Mikuni carbs, and a set of high-compression pistons. Just what the doctor ordered. Those were definitely the good old days!"

Around 1974, Sarge got into sandrails and enjoyed hitting the dunes whenever the opportunity arose. "It was Harvey Weidman's influence (as well as his brother's) that got me interested in building a sandrail," he recalls. "I remember that first trip to the dunes before I'd built a car, and being 'hooked'. The 'group' at the dunes included Don Bradford (Brad's Upholstery), Dean Kirsten, Mike Martin and his wife, Julie (who had bought Dean's blue '67 Bug), as well as Harvey's brother Al and Al Noriega (my old boss from Renfree Motors). I finished my first Buggy, which ran a 2074cc motor, around 1977 and *Hot VWs* magazine featured it a short time later. In 1984, it was replaced with a second Buggy, with a mid-engined 2332cc."

It was in the mid-1970s that Sarge experi-

enced what he called "burn-out", which was hardly surprising considering how many years he had been active in the VW club and racing scene. "I could probably write a book on this topic! My 'burn-out' came from too much time at the drags – the wait in the staging lanes, the missed shift, the lost race, driving back and forth from the track with close-ratio gears on the freeway, you name it. So, when the first generation DKP folded in the early 1970s, I still had an urge, but wanted to be as far away as possible from the restrictions of a drag strip, which is something I still feel the same about today. The sand dunes at Glamis welcomed my wife and I for the next 20 years – there were no more rules,

Single quiet-pack muffler is perhaps the only detail which dates this photograph of Edmiston's late-model sedan. Everything else would like right at home in SoCal today. (Jim Edmiston)

On returning from Vietnam, Sarge had to get his priorities right. First buy a new Volkswagen, then marry your fiancée… (Jim Edmiston)

ulcers or regulations, just loads of new friends and plenty of stress-free excitement behind the wheel of a lightweight, scary-fast rail. I still had a Bug, but I never went to the track, Bug-Ins, or any of the other shows."

In the five years Sarge spent working in Riverside at the dealership, Darrell Vittone was responsible for his coming to meet a lot of interesting characters – and one was Chas Morse. Vittone had grown tired of Econo Motors and finally pulled out to start Techtonics (developing and selling parts for water-cooled VWs), which was located in a small complex with Richard McPeek (the famous race car painter and the man responsible for many of the top race cars of the day, such as the *Deano Dyno Soar*). Sand-

The '69 was first fitted with a 1776cc engine with dual Kadron carbs, but ended its days with a 2017cc motor with dual 48IDA Webers. It was eventually destroyed by a drunk driver. (Jim Edmiston)

wiched between them was Chas Morse's metal fabrication shop.

Sarge recalls: "I'm pretty sure Chas was responsible for building some of the very first merged-collector VW exhaust systems. He was a real artist at metal fabrication and a pleasure to spend time with. He was always working on cool stuff, too. When I was building my first sandrail, it was Chas who built the carb linkage, the breather box and a unique flat collector exhaust system. The price was always right and you could always count on hearing some good stories while he was building your stuff. Sadly, Chas passed away from spinal cancer sometime in the 1980s at a relatively young age.

"When I started at Sierra, in early 1973, I had the Datsun truck, as well as a 1969 Beetle my wife and I had bought new at Don Burns VW when I got home from the Army. We used it for travelling and my wife, Sharon, used it for commuting back and forth to work. I had little interest back then in the '69 – until the fall of 1973, when Porsche debuted the new-look 1974 models. Harvey suggested that I 'Porsche-ize' the car with some black trim, as the new Carreras came with blacked-out trim round the windows.

"Back then, we did loads of wheel swap upgrades, and I was able to snag a set of Mahle 914 alloys for just $25 each. Also, VW had a number of special-edition cars at the time (Sun Bug, Jeans Bug, etc) that came from the factory with black trim, so I set about ordering all the pieces from Volkswagen. As for the engine, I built a 1776 with an Engle 110 camshaft and 041 cylinder heads. It was about this time that the first Solex-Kadron carburettor kits were just coming out, so I got a set of those to try.

"The suspension received a new front beam with adjusters, a full set of Koni shocks and three-quarter-inch Sway-A-Way anti-roll bars front and rear. I fitted Pirelli Cinturato tyres, using 185/70s on the rear and 195/60s on the front. Needless to say, this car handled great and made for an awesome road car for many years, taking us all over California, Oregon and Arizona. I eventually upgraded the engine to 2017cc, with 48IDA Weber carburettors. We certainly had some fun times back then, but the car was totalled outside our house one day in 1993, when a drunk driver drove straight into the back of it. The impact was so hard that it pushed the crankshaft forward through the motor into the trans. We were heartbroken," Sarge recalls.

"When my Datsun pick-up was stolen in 1984 from the VW dealership where I was working, a 1967 Beetle in the used car lot became mine.

My 're-light' came around 1998, courtesy of Keith Seume, when I read the original *California Look VW* book, something for which I will always be grateful. Oddly enough, I bought that '67 solely for transportation, without any thought of Cal Looking it – but, when push came to shove, old habits die hard. My feeling is that much of what happens nowadays has a lot to do with what's been written about the good old days, in books, magazines and Internet forums."

It was inevitable, really, that the Edmistons' "new" Beetle wouldn't stay stock for long. In 1989, the by-now dechromed body was resprayed a special blend of bright red paint by Becker's Bug House, the business responsible for painting many of the classic California Look cars of old, including Greg Aronson's seminal white 1963 sedan. Turning to the inside, Sarge then entrusted Ernie Yanez Jr, of Quality Auto Upholstery, with the task of copying the "Fat Biscuit" stitching, made famous by Brad's Upholstery. This was complemented by a LeCarra steering wheel, AutoMeter tachometer and a Gene Berg gear shifter.

Sarge continues the story: "I built my current 2017cc motor in 2000 and have covered in the region of 16,000 miles with no problems. It was built with reliability in mind, as the crank is a bit of an antique (it's an original Tony Mance welded 78.4mm stroker) that was gifted to me by Doug Mische.

I chose to use an Engle 125 cam, as it's the one around which I based a lot of my earlier motors, and it has always served me well. The heads were ported by Fumio Fukaya and use 40mm x 35.5mm valves and dual springs, while the rockers are 1.1:1 with Porsche 911 swivel-feet adjusters. The carburettors are Weber 48IDAs, which came courtesy of Ron Fleming, who salvaged them off an alcohol-burning sandrail. When I tore them apart, every jet, tube and orifice had to be cleaned out or replaced, as they had all been bored out to the max for use with alcohol.

"My plan is to build a 2332cc, Engle K8 combination some day – we'll see what happens! For the time being, the gearbox retains stock gears, as the car was meant to be street-driven extensively, but transmission builder (and fellow DKP club member) Jim Kaforski heavily beefed up the unit and added Sway-A-Way short

axles. The same company supplied the uprated 24mm torsion bars, in addition to the adjustable spring plates."

To further improve drivability, Sarge has also installed larger Type 3 brake drums at the rear, with German-made CSP disc brakes at the front, mounted on CB Performance dropped spindles and a two-inch narrowed beam with adjusters.

It's been over 40 years since Jim Edmiston first got behind the wheel of a Volkswagen – and almost as long since he first drove a modified one. Somehow, one can't help but get the feeling that people like Sarge never quite grow up – and long may it be so.

This, after all, is what the California Look experience is really all about.

When Jim became "burned-out" with the Cal Look scene, he decided to build a sandrail, with A-arm front suspension and healthy 2332cc motor. (Jim Edmiston)

Jim's current ride is this bright red '67, with a 2017cc engine running Fumio Fukaya heads. (Jim Edmiston)

Chapter 3

THE FASTEST BUG IN TOWN

"You can't drive this on the street. It has more horsepower than the Inch Pincher did a year ago!"
Mike Mahaffey

1960s

Mike Mahaffey's 1951 Split-window Bug looked innocent enough but looks could be deceiving. Among the first changes Mahaffey made to the car was to fit a set of chromed Porsche wheels and a one-off exhaust system. (Mike Mahaffey)

"That was a fun time, you know, the height of the muscle car era. The cruise scene was centred on Harbor Boulevard in Anaheim, heading between Big Carl's and Taco Villa – it was like a scene straight out of the film *American Graffiti*. We were the anti-muscle car crowd that was basically laughed at…"

The words of Mike Mahaffey perfectly sum up the SoCal street scene in the late 1960s and early 1970s. Cruising – basically the parading of your car before an impromptu but usually apprecia-

tive audience – was the fun way to spend your Friday or Saturday night. Owners of hot rods, customs and the growing ranks of Detroit-built muscle cars would meet up in the parking lot of one or other of the popular burger joints, or ice-cream parlours, to show off their latest rides. Most cruises were little more than mobile displays of cool cars, with even cooler dudes – and their chicks – behind the wheel. Most, but not all.

It is pretty much a foregone conclusion that, if you assemble enough such vehicles, the question of who's got the fastest car in town will soon rear its head. And there was only one way to find out. If you watched the aforementioned film, *American Graffiti*, then you could easily be led to believe that you'd need a stripped-out '55 Chevy, or a "piss-yellow" '32 Ford coupe, to win "fastest car in town" bragging rights. Few people would bet on a VW Bug being the King of the Hill. And that line of thinking would prove to be the downfall of many an owner of a highly-tuned V8 muscle car…

Mike Mahaffey's innocent-looking 1951 Split-window Beetle was, without doubt, a major contender for the title King of the Hill. It was the perfect sleeper, its vintage styling belying the fact that it ran a high-compression VW "stroker" engine and close-ratio gears – and was capable of low 13-second times over the quarter-mile. That made it far quicker than most showroom-stock muscle cars.

The car began life in Mahaffey's hands as a dark brown sedan which had been "updated"

with later tail lights and front turn signals. Under his ownership, the car soon began to change, sporting a set of widened chrome Porsche-style steel rims mounted on gold-painted brake drums, as was the fashion in the mid- to late-1960s. The car also carried a set of full bumpers with export "towel-rail" bumper guards and, for a while at least, a large-diameter tailpipe mounted to an extractor exhaust header.

It didn't remain looking this way for long, as the owner had other ideas. Leonard Becker painted the car 1970 Porsche Conda Green and, although the bodywork was dechromed at this point, the decision was made to retain the slots in the fenders for the bumpers, just in case they needed to be refitted at a later date (running without bumpers was a ticketable offence). A set of lightweight BRM magnesium wheels also replaced the chromed rims. A set of VDO gauges was installed in the otherwise stock dashboard and the interior was treated to a retrim, too, with the stock seats reupholstered in black "fat biscuit" style.

"I was working at an upholstery supply warehouse during college, and an auto upholsterer customer of ours from Fullerton did the work," recalls Mahaffey. "I chose him because he cut me a good deal and he was good at his work. It was during my employment there that I met another upholsterer, Don Bradford, and introduced him to the VW scene." Bradford – known better simply as "Brad" – became the trimmer of choice within the California Look scene for years to come.

Before Mahaffey built his car, what were considered to be fast street VWs ran high 15-second or low 16-second quarter-mile times. "They were hardly a threat to muscle car owners," he recalls. "The really fast cars were built purely for drag racing – cars like the *Inch Pincher* and the Schley Brothers' *Lightning Bug*. I didn't know of anybody who'd made that kind of technology work on the street, let alone in a daily-driven VW!" The latter point is an important one for, as we shall see, few VW enthusiasts

BRM wheels became the rim of choice in the late 1960s, especially among those seeking ultimate performance. They were lighter than stock but stronger than race-only spun-aluminium rims. (Mike Mahaffey)

couldn't afford one of those. I was just a college student still going to school full time and working only part time, so I had very little money available. What I did have I spent on my car, leaving just a little over for beer at our club rallies."

That engine was fast, but fragile, ending its days by disintegrating halfway down the Lions drag strip at Long Beach, California. "Plan B" was to build a 2180cc engine based around an 82mm SPG roller-bearing crankshaft and a set of NPR 92mm cylinders and pistons. "I couldn't afford to blow up another motor. This car was my only transportation, and if it broke on Sunday I didn't have a ride to school on Monday. Our cars were not toys – they were all we had, so they got driven everywhere on a daily basis. So I guess my building such a big motor was taking a risk for a 'daily driver' – a term, incidentally, which we never used at the time."

Mahaffey and fellow club member Ron Fleming, who was also responsible for modifying the dual-port cylinder heads with D-shaped inlet ports, built the new motor. The heads were equipped with 40mm inlet valves, but retained the stock exhaust valves purely because Mahaffey couldn't afford any extra work. The camshaft was an Engle 130 grind, with dual 48IDA Weber carburettors and a

of the time were in the fortunate position of owning more than one vehicle.

Mahaffey talked the subject over with fellow DKP club members and decided, in his own words, "to go for it". The first engine he ran in the car was a 2074cc "stroker" with a welded, non-counterweighted 78mm crankshaft. "About the only thing available then – other than the welded ones – were forged Okrasa cranks, but I

"After a full pull on the dyno, Dean Lowry just looked at us and told us we were crazy. 'You can't drive this on the street. It has more horsepower than the Inch Pincher did a year ago!' We smiled, and said: 'We'll see.'" (Mike Mahaffey)

Vertex magneto. "It ran great on the street, a real torquer, better than anyone thought it would. Gene Berg machined some special close-ratio third and fourth gears to go with the ZF limited-slip differential I was running. With the solid steel mounts and no sound deadening, it was unbelievably noisy. I couldn't even hear my eight-track stereo, so I decided I might as well take it out!"

Mahaffey had the engine run on a dynamometer by Dean Lowry. "After a full pull he just looked at us and told us we were crazy. 'You can't drive this on the street. It has more horsepower than the *Inch Pincher* did a year ago!' We just smiled, and said: 'We'll see.' Actually, it worked far better than we had even dared to hope. It was a torque monster that pulled all the way from idle. Looking back, I'm sure the Vertex magneto helped a lot." In fact, the engine made a truly impressive 192bhp with the fan belt on, and 198bhp with it removed.

The weakness as far as most heavyweight VWs were concerned was always the transmission but, by limiting the tyre size, Mahaffey avoided the breakages that have beset so many fast street-driven VWs over the years. "I only ran Pirelli radials, rather than race slicks, and came off the line at only about 3500rpm, as I wanted to make sure I didn't break the transmission or twist the SPG roller crank. Even so, the car still ran in the low 13s – and I drove it to school the next day!"

Jim Edmiston recalls taking a ride in the innocent-looking Split-window Bug: "With all the current speed parts and big horsepower of today, it's hard to truly appreciate Mike's accomplishments of so long ago. I took an all too short ride in his car when it had the 2180cc engine and clearly remember how it literally blew those

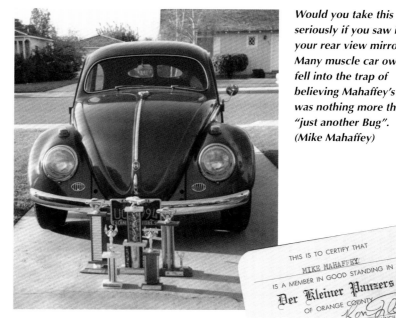

Would you take this car seriously if you saw it in your rear view mirror? Many muscle car owners fell into the trap of believing Mahaffey's VW was nothing more than "just another Bug".
(Mike Mahaffey)

Don't you just love the wording on the Der Kleiner Panzers membership card?
(Mike Mahaffey)

Word soon began to spread about Mahaffey's Split-window and wherever the car went it provoked interest. It's seen here in the staging lanes at Orange County International Raceway surrounded by an anticipatory crowd.
(Mike Mahaffey)

Around 1970, the Split-window underwent a major make-over. Leonard Becker at Becker's Bug House removed the factory trim and repainted the car Porsche Conda Green. The turn signals were replaced by US-spec units from an Oval-window Bug. (Mike Mahaffey)

VDO gauges were installed in the Split-window dash pods. Note the original turn signal switch has been retained. Two-spoke steering wheel was an unusual choice. (Mike Mahaffey)

poor Pirellis away – and how easily the back end stepped sideways as he shifted into second. Then there were those close-ratio gears… It was all unbelievable back then!"

Mahaffey realised that he now owned a major contender in the street-racing stakes although, as most of his fellow club members concur, the racing was mainly for bragging rights, rather than the big money that some people raced –

and died – for up in parts of Los Angeles. "Suddenly, I had a legitimate low 13-second street car, with fan belt, muffler, and those skinny little Pirelli tyres. Most of the muscle cars were forced to run slicks to gain any traction on the street, and would uncork the exhaust headers when things got serious. None of these guys had ever seen a fast street-driven Volkswagen before and didn't take us seriously." This attitude would

Late night pit action at OCIR. Mahaffey (with back to camera) removes the fanbelt prior to another run. That simple trick was good for around seven more horsepower – every little helps. (Mike Mahaffey)

With its Pirelli-clad BRM wheels, dechromed bodywork and nose-down stance, Mahaffey's Bug exhibited the classic elements of the original California Look style. Note the single glasspack muffler tucked under the rear apron. (Mike Mahaffey)

prove to be the downfall of many a muscle car owner…

"I remember driving through the parking lot at the back of Big Carl's in Anaheim and seeing a guy in a Chevy Chevelle with his head out of the window, laughing at my car. That was it! I backed up, bounced the front end up and down a little and then did a major burnout, before lifting the front wheels off the ground a good few inches. I drove back around the lot and stopped in front of his car, yelling out: 'So, you want to race that piece of s#*t?' The look on his face was priceless as he slumped down in his seat while all his friends stood around laughing at him!" Score one to the Bug…

On another occasion, Mahaffey recalls how he was out cruising alone one night on Harbor Boulevard in La Habra. "I pulled up next to a 1968 Mustang fastback. He was obviously very proud of his car, as he still had his dial-in time of 11.85 written in white shoe polish on his windshield, presumably a memento from his last Wednesday night bracket racing session at Orange County raceway. So, naturally, I revved

him off.

"He and his passenger just looked across at me and started laughing – obviously they didn't take the Bug very seriously, either. Instead, he ignored me and just nailed it. I stayed a half a car behind before punching the throttle and lunging ahead of him. I'll never forget the looks of disbelief on their faces as I screamed past. We pulled up to the next intersection and now he

The 1960's tail lights were swapped for Oval-window "heart" lights. Note how the bumper-iron slots in the rear fenders were retained, even though bumpers were never refitted. (Mike Mahaffey)

Door trim panels looked especially stylish, with their "fat biscuit" inserts and carpeted kick panel along the bottom edge. One-piece window glass was stock in 1951 – and perfect for "the Look" . (Mike Mahaffey)

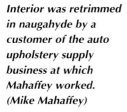

Interior was retrimmed in naugahyde by a customer of the auto upholstery supply business at which Mahaffey worked. (Mike Mahaffey)

knew I was serious. I sat and watched the lights at the intersection, trying to anticipate the green. We both took off, smoking the tyres away from the line. I eventually shut it down when the speedo hit 100mph, by which time I'd had him by about two car lengths. I turned one way while

The clocks never lie – OCIR's timing equipment recorded this 13.24-second pass at 99mph. Not the car's quickest, but still impressive. (Mike Mahaffey)

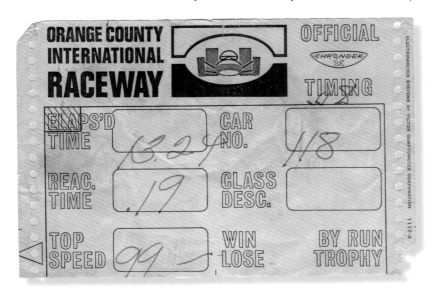

he turned the other, splitting up in case a cop happened to see us. I would have loved to have heard the conversation in the Mustang after that little display!"

The story of the "lil green Bug" soon spread, and the car began to take on almost legendary status in the street-racing fraternity. Mahaffey turned up one night at the local Taco Villa, minus his car. "I approached a crowd engaged in some animated story telling. I stood back and listened while they talked about an 11-second street VW. That got my interest and I began wondering where the heck is that car. I didn't know of any Volkswagens that were that fast! Then one of the guys in the crowd that knew me whispered: 'They're talking about your car.' I couldn't get any more races from those muscle car guys after that episode!"

Eventually, it came time for the car and owner to go their separate ways. The Split-window was sold, minus its stroker engine, to Ed Craig, who considers the day he bought it as one of the best in his life "...and years later one of my biggest mistakes was selling it!" he ruefully recalls. "When I bought the car, it was with the intention of never selling it, but when I was offered what seemed to me like big bucks at the time, that did the trick."

The car appeared in *Volkswagen Greats*

magazine in 1974 while in Craig's hands. By this time, it sported a 1600cc engine with a 300cfm Holley Bugspray carburettor on an Autohaus manifold, Bosch 010 distributor, EMPI full-flow oil pump and an S&S exhaust header. It also still wore a set of BRM wheels. This spec was later upgraded to an 1800cc motor with dual 48IDA Webers on short Race Trim manifolds.

"Actually, it was the BRMs that ultimately led me to sell it. At the time, you could buy a used set for around $200, but some guy offered me $500 for mine, so it didn't take too much effort to make the decision to sell them. I put chrome wheels on the car until I could find another set of BRMs, and then someone offered to buy the car. I never liked it with the chrome wheels, so it seemed like selling was a good idea."

The new owner, Tony de Kruiff, didn't appear to have the same feeling for the Bug and made some changes that totally altered the car's persona. Ed Craig was not impressed: "The guy I sold it to put gold EMPI eight-spokes on it. I'm not judging anyone on their taste, but gold eight-spokes on a green car sure didn't work for me!" The Split-window appeared in the launch issue of *VW Trends* magazine in this guise. The new owner only kept it for about a year or two before selling it to someone who worked at the Hanna Barbara film studios. What happened to it after that is unknown, although Craig believes he may have seen it for sale at the renowned Pomona swap meet some years later, by which time it

had been repainted red.

Before we leave the Conda Green Split-window and its tales of street-racing glory, we ought to highlight one other "fifteen minutes of fame" in the car's illustrious history. Ed Craig tells the tale… "In a kids' book, there's a picture of my car at Disneyland. I was there for the première of the film *Herbie the Love Bug*, and the car had to be 'in costume'. So I painted whitewalls on my tyres using shoe whitener, let all the air out of my front shocks, hung some green "dingle balls" in the windows, taped on some flames… you get the idea. It looked so bad, I was actually embarrassed to drive it down to Disneyland!"

Perhaps not quite on the same level as a tale of street racing an 11-second Mustang, but fun all the same… It would be great to think this car might still be alive and kicking somewhere in the world. Maybe it's been restored? Who knows.

Mahaffey took the 2074cc engine to Dean Lowry to run on his dynamometer. The results were 191.8bhp at 6000rpm with the fanbelt on, and 198.1bhp with the belt removed. Extremely impressive readings for any street-driven VW, let alone one built almost 40 years ago. Later 2180cc engine almost certainly produced more power. (Mike Mahaffey)

The classic square-panelled seat trim gave a stylish look to the car. Details such as the black dash inserts and colour-coded steering column helped the overall effect. (Mike Mahaffey)

Chapter 4
MEMORIES OF HAPPIER TIMES

"No responsibilities, no mortgage, no kids, friends to hang around with, time to kill, weekends off to go wherever you want."
Dave Dolan

1960s

Chevrolet rims on VW centres allowed the use of Goodyear Blue Streak tyres, but resulted in the sidewalls being exposed outside the fenders. Narrow Porsche front rims wore skinny radials. (Ron Fleming)

"The first VW I had was actually my mom's old blue Beetle. I didn't set out to buy one but my mom bought it and I picked out the colour, but I think she didn't like it. Instead, she bought another car – so I got the Beetle and took over the payments." Dave Dolan, a member of the original Der Kleiner Panzers VW Club, remembers his formative years in the VW scene with a faraway look in his eyes.

"My dad had owned a Volkswagen before, but my first car was 1953 Ford, for which I paid $25 from a guy I used to work with. It threw a rod soon after I bought it! I had a couple of other cars before I got the VW – that was probably my third car. It was a '67 sedan – first year of 12-volt electrics, which was a great improvement. Most of the guys' cars still had the old six-volt systems. Eight-track stereos were really popular – but when they drove up to a stop light, their tapes would slow down!"

Dave Dolan went to high school with DKP founder member Pete Dayton. "We started hanging around together and only then found out we both had Bugs." The first modifications were simple in the extreme: "We'd start out by taking off all the dash-knobs and putting wooden ones in their place. Then we'd get a chrome ashtray and stuff like that. At the time, I was hanging around mostly with Jim Holmes and Don Crane, and they were into racing – especially Don, as he had the money to do it. So I kind of got into that way of thinking, little by little.

"When I rebuilt the engine for my car, I was working at a Pontiac dealership in Anaheim. They had a programme where, if you needed work done on your motor, you could get it done and they would charge it to your account so you could pay it off in instalments. I had a cam put in it, the heads machined, ported and polished, and had the crank balanced – we used to take all our stuff up to Gardenia, El Segundo or Long Beach for the work. I had a set of exhaust headers put on by Pat, at Anchor Headers, who used to do a lot of them for the club guys.

The prospect of being drafted into the military was forever in the mind of any young male growing up in the 1960s, and the consequences of this affected club members in a variety of ways – some good, some not so… "Greg Bunch was one of the first to go into the services. He saw what was going on and joined the Air Force, so I bought the tyres and rims off his car. They were Goodyear Blue Streaks – although I didn't race with them, I always thought they looked perfect," says Dolan. "In my mind, the back of the car looked really good, with a single exhaust pipe and a big megaphone-style muffler in white. My '67 was a great car for cruising as it sounded just right. It wasn't fast like Don Crane's but I didn't have the money to do everything. Don had fitted dual-port heads and had the first set of 48IDA Webers, whereas I just had a two-barrel Holley. It still used to run high 17s or low 18s, though."

Clearly, the design of the exhaust system was of paramount importance to club members: "Mufflers? I had a set of duals on the car first of all, but didn't like them, or the lack of horse-power. That's when I went down to Pat (Anchor Mufflers) and told him what I wanted. It made a big difference to the horsepower. The (club) members had a lot of different types of muffler specially built for them, and you could tell different people's cars from the way they sounded coming down the street!

"The club wasn't as organised then as it became later. A lot of the guys would just get together for fun – remember, back then gas was only 30 cents a gallon! We would drive out to Palm Springs and cruise up and down the avenues. We raced an old 1600 Datsun out there one time and I was the only guy who won his race. I just took off the muffler and fan-belt and raced for five bucks!"

Dolan recalls how street racing was a big deal back in the 1960s, and definitely not just among the VW crowd. "There was plenty of horsepower around then – 396 Chevelles, big-block Fords and the like. They used to race a lot in the Anaheim area. All the 'hot stuff' in town used to cruise through Carl's drive-in to show off a new car – or a new girlfriend! All the cars were polished up and it was a chance to see who was new in the area, and who had got what.

"DKP really got into street racing, but only the hardcore of members like myself, Don Crane, Ron Fleming, Greg Aronson, Jim Holmes, Ron

Brimlow and Bob Moore started to concentrate on it. I remember Don and Ron especially! There was a lot of good stuff coming out, such as the dual-port heads, new cams, etc.

"I joined the military in 1968 when it (street racing) was really taking off. The two years I was gone, from 1968 to '70, was when the quantum leap took place. There were a lot of wide-open areas around then: Nabisco factory, La Palma

Dolan poses with the 1967 Beetle he acquired from his mother. (Ron Fleming)

"Race car in tow" was worn like a badge of honour on the Freeway. (Ron Fleming)

Carlsbad Raceway drew Dolan and fellow club members like moths to a flame. It was certainly no high-class facility but it offered plenty of opportunities to race. (Jim Edmiston)

Avenue (way out of town there was a great four-lane stretch), behind the Kimberley Clark factory… Around Carl's was another spot – a meat-packing plant. One night I was racing another VW down there but the place was getting too well known. A cop was sitting there waiting for us while we were racing. As I went shooting by, the cop pulled out and I pulled over, but he went after the other guy. I did a quick U-turn and headed home!"

Dolan recalls the club days with affection: "Some meetings were a real riot. There was always a big debate about whether to let girls into the club. It became very heated because one guy really liked this girl – Sue Miller – who had a VW, but they wouldn't let her in. I don't know if I was president then, or Chuck Henry – he was married and his wife used to come along.

"I remember best of all helping to organise the rallies – laying out new courses, timing them to get instructions right, working check points, organising plaques and trophies. The club used to have rallies to help make money to be able to buy more trophies and pay rent on the club-

In Dolan's time with Der Kleiner Panzers, there was a tremendous feeling of camaraderie and everyone got a real kick out of driving their VWs hard and fast. Ron Fleming's Oval-window was one of the best-looking cars in the club. (Ron Fleming)

house. DKP members were close to the Santa Ana club. We would caravan together down to Mexico and some of the guys would surf. We also used to caravan up to Hollywood to Sunset Boulevard – Hollywood was a great place back then – or to Palm Springs, which was about a two-hour drive. We rarely just drove aimlessly – caravans usually had a destination.

"I used to go to watch drag racing at Lions before I joined the club and participated once I was a member. Club cars would tow each other to the strip – there was a lot of kudos associated with driving down the freeway with cars in tow! We would take out seats and take off bumpers, remove the fan-belt and spare wheel, and change the exhaust for a stinger. I used to go to Pomona and Irwindale a lot with Don Crane, and then to Orange County.

"I went to high school with Pete Dayton, although I didn't want to know him then! But after I got in the club, I found out that Steve Harf had graduated just a year after me. It seems like the whole club developed out of this group. Jim Mawhar had an older step-brother, Bob Foust, who had a bunch of friends, and after I came out of the Army I hung around with them and Darrell Vittone (of EMPI). Many of them had been to the same high schools, principally around Anaheim. We were like brothers and there was a great feeling of camaraderie."

But life has a habit of catching up with everybody, and it soon became time for Dave Dolan to think about the future. "Back then, the club was my whole life. I had already graduated from high school, so I went after a job at North American Aviation, but they wouldn't hire me. So I

Known as "The Sweatbox", the entry booth at Carlsbad Raceway was taken over by DKP members at the club's Drag Day events. (Jim Edmiston)

Dolan (centre, front) and friends with his as-yet unlowered Beetle. Chromed Porsche rims were a popular addition. (Ron Fleming)

Dave Dolan recalls there being a lot of kudos attached to flat-towing a Bug on the Freeway. Doug Gordon's Underdog is shown waiting in line in the entry road to Carlsbad. (Ron Fleming)

43

When Greg Bunch left home to join the US Air Force, he sold the Goodyear Blue Streak tyres and chrome rims from his car (right) to Dave Dolan. Blue Streaks offered little grip but users reported they squealed easily and looked cool! (Greg Bunch)

Stopping to check tyre pressures on the way to the strip – Dolan's '67 is being flat-towed behind fellow club member's VW Microbus. (Ron Fleming)

just continued hanging out, just lying around at home, until I got drafted.

"Whenever that happened, the club would have a going-away party then all go to the bus station to see the draftee off. Lots of club guys were getting drafted and I remember seeing off Steve Harf, Steve Stow, Chuck Henry and Bob Moore, who was killed in Vietnam – I got called

up the same day as Bob, but didn't weigh enough for my height! I stayed out for another year-and-a half-but was called up finally in 1968 for six months – they needed bodies for Vietnam, I guess. I used to eat salads to keep my weight down whenever I went out with club!

"I'd graduated in '65 when I was 18, and should have been drafted at 19 or 20, but didn't get called up until I was 21. In fact, I was probably one of last members to go into the draft – some had already come back by the time I went in. At least a third to a half of members got drafted. I lost touch with the club during my two years away, and when I came home there were lots of new faces and a different scene. I'd met several people in the services who were interested in VWs, but not in the same way that DKP members were."

When he returned from Germany, Dolan found many things had changed. "Being in the service for two years really affects you. I only went to about one party and one club meeting after I came back. That was the last real contact I had with rest of the guys. The club just wasn't an important thing in my life any more. I was 23 when I got out and had been through lots of different experiences when in the forces – I felt I just didn't fit in any more. I wasn't into cars so much – my life went in a different direction. The

days spent with DKP? No question, they were a terrific time in my life. No responsibilities, no mortgage, no kids, friends to hang around with, time to kill, weekends off to go wherever you want. After I came out of the Army, I went back to school for a while, but I dropped out and went to join friends over in the islands."

For Dave Dolan, like many others of his generation, the VW experience played a major role in life – but sometimes life itself has a habit of getting in the way.

A distant war in far-off Asia, the draft, seeing friends go away and never return… When all is said and done, while playing with cars can be fun, it's the friendships you make along the way that matter the most.

Carlsbad Raceway's famous mobile home-cum-office looks down on the startline as Don Crane blasts off on another 13-second pass. DKP Drag Days were popular and attracted many of the serious race cars of the day. (Ron Fleming)

Chapter 5

CALIFORNIA LOOK COMES OF AGE

"I don't ever want to see this car going that fast on my road again – is that clear?"

1970s

The February 1975 issue of Hot VWs *magazine was the first to give this new breed of fast Volkswagens media recognition. Jim Holmes is shown polishing his white rag-top sedan. (Author's collection)*

By the time the 1970s arrived, what would later become recognised as the "California Look" was beginning to evolve. To begin with, the "Look" was almost exclusively associated with the Der Kleiner Panzers VW Club from Anaheim, but it didn't take long before others followed suit. However, it was a style which remained somewhat surprisingly unrecognised by the media for several more years.

There was plenty going on in the 1970s, a decade which author Tom Wolfe referred to as the "Me decade", for it seemed that everyone (well, those under the age of 40) was hell-bent on exploiting hedonism to the full. Sex, drugs and rock 'n' roll were the order of the day – at least, in some quarters of the USA. Music was undergoing a serious period of change once more, with artists like Neil Young, CSNY (Crosby, Stills, Nash and Young), Pink Floyd, Led Zeppelin and Deep Purple maturing musically and becoming almost household names alongside The Beatles, The Rolling Stones and other '60s icons. The days of the crooner were long gone…

And then along came Punk Rock, thumbing its nose at convention and showing little or no respect for whatever had gone before. Bands such as the Sex Pistols, The Clash and, in the USA, the Ramones, turned conventional musical wisdom on its head – just like those California Look Volkswagens were doing on the streets and strips of southern California. As far as the "old school" muscle car guys were concerned, this new breed of high-powered Volkswagen was the automotive equivalent of the punk generation.

Elsewhere in the world, though, there were more serious matters to attend to, as the Vietnam War continued to call upon the services of the youth of America. Richard Nixon, elected President in 1969, sought to alter the course of the war by pursuing a withdrawal strategy that led to the term "Vietnamization" being coined by the media. Until then, it had been widely felt that it was only US personnel who were dying in the conflict, and Nixon's strategy was to not only encourage the South Vietnamese army to lead the conflict, but also to seek the assistance of superpowers such as Russia and China, both of whom were supplying aid to the North Vietnamese, in bringing about a solution.

The conflict came to a somewhat inglorious end in 1975, some two years after the signing of the Paris Peace Accord by US Secretary of State Henry Kissinger, communist leader Le Duc Tho and South Vietnam's President Thieu. It was a war that had left an indelible mark on many a young American, changing people's lives and outlooks for ever.

There were other significant (if not ultimately as life-changing) events in the 1970s that had a lasting effect on VW enthusiasts across California: the smog laws. In 1967, the California Air Resources Board (CARB) was formed following the merging of the California Motor Vehicle Pollution Control Board and the Bureau of Air Sanitation, after which California State Governor Ronald Reagan signed the Mulford-Carrell Air Resources Act into law. This led directly to the Federal Air Quality Act of 1967, which established a framework for defining "air quality control regions" based on meteorological and topographical factors affecting air pollution.

The Act allowed the State of California to set and enforce its own emissions standards for new vehicles, based on the State's unique need for more stringent controls. Smog, in Los Angeles especially, was becoming a major problem and,

Ken Jevec's Oval-window typified the look of the early 1970s – not every car had lowered front suspension back then. Dechromed bodywork and chromed Porsche rims are timeless.
(Ken Jevec)

A smiling Jim Holmes holds up the very same T-shirt he wore over 30 years ago in the Hot VWs *photograph shown opposite.*
(Author)

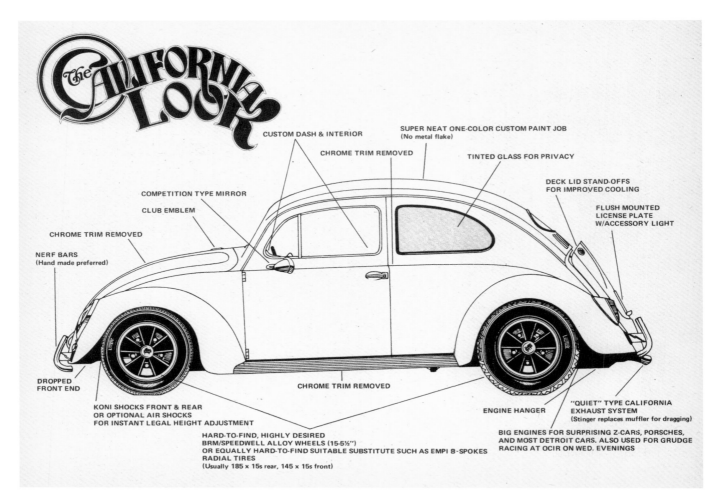

Featured in the February 1975 Hot VWs, this artwork by Lane Evans, based on an idea by Burly Burlile, demonstrated the principles of California Look style. (Author's collection)

Never before published, this is the original pen and ink drawing by Burly Burlile which acted as a basis for Lane Evans' seminal artwork. (Hot VWs)

by 1975, the first cars were being fitted with two-way catalytic converters in an effort to cut down on exhaust emissions. This instantly made it illegal to modify any new vehicle in such a way that the emissions were increased. Suddenly, late-model Beetles became even less desirable… But it didn't stop people from hot-rodding older Volkswagens.

The car which is generally regarded as the progenitor of the "Look" is the white 1963 rag-top sedan owned by Greg Aronson, of FAT Performance. With its classic nose-down stance, dechromed bodywork, BRM wheels and dual-carbed motor, to this day Aronson's Volkswagen remains firmly imprinted on everyone's memory as the car that started it all.

Strictly speaking, though, one could argue that this isn't really the case, as the California Look evolved over a period of years, starting with the first hot VWs built in Orange County in the mid-1960s – it didn't start at any one moment in time. But there is no denying that Aronson's car did have that certain *je ne sais quoi* that set it apart from the crowd. It was devoid of any fancy frills and looked like it meant business. To use Dutch architect Mies van der Rohe's oft-quoted mantra, "Less is more…".

There has been much debate in recent years

In May 1976, Keith Goss blew everybody's minds when he debuted his roof-chopped Bug at Bug-In 16. It was awarded Best of Show. (Ron Fleming)

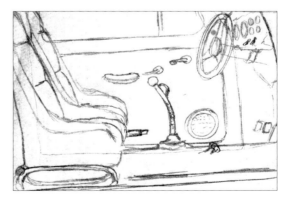

Burly Burlile's pencil sketch of the interior was intended to accompany the drawing shown opposite. (Hot VWs)

The original Lane Evans artwork for the February 1975 Hot VWs feature. (Hot VWs)

Looking very purposeful with its blacked-out trim and tinted windows, Ken Jevec's rejuvinated Oval-window wore a set of Center Line wheels. Note the lowered rear suspension, too – a relative rarity in the '70s. (Ken Jevec)

about what constitutes a true California Look sedan, but in reality it all comes down to a matter of personal taste. Most people's image of a traditional "Looker" is generally derived from the artwork drawn by Burly Burlile for *Hot VWs* magazine, and used in its seminal February 1975 issue – the first ever reference in print to the term "California Look".

Burlile's original pen-and-ink illustration shows an Oval-window sedan with radial-shod BRM wheels, nerf bars (as opposed to the widely accepted T-bars), tinted rear side glass,

Phil Kelly got the "bug" after meeting up with Jim Edmiston and eventually worked at Auto Haus, the leading VW parts retailer in Orange County. Kelly's Porsche-rimmed sedan ran a Weber-equipped 1835cc motor. (Jim Edmiston)

Built originally by Greg Aronson of Fleming & Aronson High Performance (later FAT Performance), Jim Holmes' 1963 sunroof sedan is regarded as the seminal California Look VW. All the elements are there: dechromed body, BRM wheels, T-bars, Lucas turn signals and a nose-down stance. (Jere Alhadeff)

dechromed bodywork and a deck lid fitted with stand-offs. In reality, this image was something of a mixture of what was going on at the time, for the tinted side glass was more popular in the late 1960s, while curved nerf-bars were rarely ever seen on a Bug, unless it was a custom, as opposed to a "no-frills" California Look sedan. Other "missing" elements included a Fram oil filter hanging from below the rear fender and one-piece door windows, both of which were becoming popular by the mid-1970s. There was no reference to the interior of the car, either,

Running a 1700cc motor with dual 48IDA Webers, Holmes' sedan was more than a match for much larger muscle cars. Black fender beading formed a stark contrast with the "appliance white" paintwork (Jere Alhadeff)

A mixture of Smiths and S&W gauges were installed in a unique Plexiglass dashboard. Double-stitched "fat biscuit" design used on the seats and door panels was a trademark of renowned upholsterer Don "Brad" Bradford. (Jere Alhadeff)

Along with the box-quilt padded panelling, Brad's work also typically included a carpetted strip along the bottom of each door panel to protect it from accidental scuffs when climbing in and out of the car. (Jere Alhadeff)

although a rough pencil sketch by Burlile showed the inside of a "Looker", but this was never reproduced in the magazine.

This sketch of the interior showed a pair of bucket-style seats mounted on what are presumably intended to be modified VW seat frames, with a Hurst trigger gear-shifter, three-spoke aftermarket steering-wheel, stereo speakers in the doors and, just visible, a bank of gauges in a filled dashboard. That was probably a pretty accurate representation of contemporary styles, although there is no indication of how Burlile envisaged the seats being trimmed. In reality, many cars still ran stock trim, but the better-detailed examples would feature velour inserts in naugahyde-trimmed stock or aftermarket seats, or maybe with "fat biscuit" detailing courtesy of Don "Brad" Bradford's skilled hands.

The only reference to the engine in Burlile's work is a curt "Big engines for surprising Z-cars (Datsun sports cars), Porsches and most Detroit cars". But what constituted a big engine back then is a far cry from what is generally regarded as such three decades later. The "hot ticket" in the early- to mid-1970s was a 1700cc motor using a set of 88mm cylinders and pistons, a stock (or maybe counterweighted) crankshaft, stock rods, an Engle 110 camshaft, ported heads with, perhaps, 40mm inlet valves, extractor exhaust with either a glass-pack or a single "quiet" muffler, a Bosch 010 distributor and a pair of 48IDA Weber carburettors. Such a combination was the backbone of the scene and, with enough compression and a close-ratio transmission, could provide the ride of a lifetime for an unsuspecting passenger.

The "primo" cars, on the other hand, might typically run an Okrasa stroker crank, Porsche 912 con-rods, skilfully reworked heads by Fumio Fukaya, an Engle 125 cam with EMPI high-ratio rocker arms, 90.5 or 92mm cylinders, Joe Hunt magneto and, of course, dual 48IDA Webers on Skat-Trak manifolds. Allied to a close-ratio transmission with a ZF limited-slip differential, this could turn a stock-bodied Bug into a low thirteen-, or high twelve-second car, no problem. Bump the compression ratio up to eleven-point-something, run high-test gas and you'd be looking at low twelves, easily.

An important aspect of the scene in the early 1970s was cruising and being a member of a club. Talk to any "survivor" from this era and it soon becomes clear that the camaraderie associated with the VW clubs was what made those times so special.

There was a lot of bravado, pride – call it what you will – involved with going out together as a club. It was felt important to put on a show wherever you went. After all, your honour was at stake. As Doug Mische, of Der Kleiner Panzers, recalls: "We loved to encourage the rumour that 'you can't get into that club if you don't run 48IDAs', even though some of the guys were running 42mm carburettors. And to support that we had a policy that worked perfectly: everywhere we went, when we arrived, every single car did a burnout entering the parking lot. It was awesome! Rallies were the best, because all the other car clubs would be there, and we could show off big time.

"As club President, Roger Grago would lead the way in his Karmann Ghia. He'd come into the parking lot, preload the transmission and light up the tyres, followed by the other (club) officers and members. Most always, the burnouts were great, primarily due to the fact that 165 radials don't hook up very much – it

Clubs tended to be very organised back in the 1970s, with membership cards and event fliers. Jim Edmiston's artwork on DKP publicity material has become legendary. (Ken Jevec/Author)

Holmes' engine is a lesson in period tuning, Orange County-style: dual 48IDA Webers on short manifolds, Bosch 010 distribuor, non-fresh-air fan-housing, Santana pulley, Bosch Blue coil and early Berg linkage. (Jere Alhadeff)

Der Renwagen Fuhrers had its own club house in Orange, which was used for club meetings but could also be rented out by individual members for their own use. (Ken Jevec)

sounded and looked terrific. I don't want to sound too proud, but I think I'm right in saying that it was no secret when DKP arrived."

Hard driving took its toll on engines, but gearboxes were notoriously the weakest link, especially back in the days before aftermarket parts were so readily available. Mische recalls his first experience of discovering the limits of a VW transmission – the hard way. "We were heading for a club rally and, as we arrived, did

Given a free hand to design rally fliers, Jim Edmiston's drawings became more and more adventurous (Author's collection)

The front window of the club house was used as a display case for members' trophies if for no other reason than to show off to rival clubs! (Ken Jevec)

burnouts coming in like always. When my turn came, I spun first gear really good, then bang-shifted into second, but missed it. I felt like such a dope. But my pals in other clubs were good sports about it and teased the shit out of me. I thought: 'That's OK, I'll make up for it when we leave,' because we did burnouts whenever we left, too.

"So I got my rally instructions, started my car and got ready to depart. I turned right into the street, nailed it hard in first and then missed second gear – again! What! Twice in a row? Never! Well, as it turns out, I hadn't missed the gear – I simply had no second gear left to miss! With the gear lever in second, I could rev the motor just like it was in neutral. In the end, I ran that rally with three gears. When I took a look inside the 'box, I found that I had sheared all the synchro teeth off second gear. Luckily, none of the debris found its way to the ring and pinion, or that would have been a real mess. I still have that gear somewhere, possibly because I knew no one would ever believe it."

Displays of horsepower took many forms, as Mische recalls with a wry smile: "One night on the 22 Freeway, I came up on a late-model Corvette – and when the guy looked over at me, he jumped on it. I could hear his carb sucking beneath the hood, so I downshifted to third and just left him, hit the redline at about 85–90mph, then hit fourth, and shut off at about 110. Unbelievably, the guy in the 'Vette tried the same

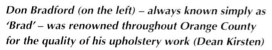

Don Bradford (on the left) – always known simply as 'Brad' – was renowned throughout Orange County for the quality of his upholstery work (Dean Kirsten)

thing again, with the exact same result. His girl-friend was now smiling at me and this guy was starting to get really pissed, and he went off again. What a moron! I can't imagine what he was thinking. So the same thing happened again – and this time, when he came past, his girlfriend was laughing pretty good, and he wasn't even willing to look over at me. I guess I was lucky that freeway shootings hadn't been thought of yet!"

Right or wrong, street racing was big – very big – in the 1970s. In some areas of Los Angeles, huge amounts of money changed hands on bets between racers. But, as far as the VW club scene was concerned, most "races" were impromptu affairs, settled at a stop light. The 1970s were the glory days of the American muscle car, but the big problem would always be that it was difficult to get a front-engined car to hook up on the street. That's where even relatively low-powered VWs scored time and time again. But when the opponent was driving another rear-engined performance car, surely the tables would be turned? Well, not necessarily so…

What Doug Mische refers to as his "very favourite street race" happened while the third gear was broken in his Karmann Ghia's gearbox. Bob Hood was a fellow parts counterman at Chick Iverson VW, where Doug worked, and he had gone over to his friend's place to hang out one night. "When we ran out of beer, we went to go get more. Bob was a die-hard Porsche lover,

and every time I told him that my Ghia would outrun a 911, even a Turbo, he would laugh hysterically and poke fun at me.

"So we took the Ghia and, as fate would have it, while we were sitting at a light on Newport Blvd, a 930 Turbo pulled up in the lane next to us. Bob said: 'OK, here's your chance – show me.' Believe it or not, the guy in the Turbo threw me a rev first, and preloaded with his handbrake (you gotta love that FASRNU licence plate!), so I

Members of DKP kick back in a local park prior to a club photoshoot. (Ron Fleming)

Even mainstream media caught the "bug" as this Los Angeles Times shows. (Author's collection)

LEAVING THE PLAIN VOLKS BEHIND

Der Renwagen Fuhrers member Mark Hunsaker owned this 1966 sedan, which was painted a deep maroon. Powered by a FAT Performance 182bhp 1940cc engine, the Bug ran a best of 12.37 seconds at 108mph in 1976. (Dean Kirsten)

did likewise. When the light went green, the Turbo left hard and actually got a hole-shot on me by maybe half a car's length. Once I got the Ghia going, I went by him in first gear like he was parked, banged second and got in front of him by about eight to ten car lengths – only then did I realize that third gear wasn't going to be worth a damn.

"I shifted into third and tried to feather it, but it started making those god-awful noises and the Turbo was coming up on us really fast. About the time his front bumper was even with my rear bumper, I short-shifted to fourth, and the Ghia

FAT Performance pioneered the use of T-bars in the 1970s. (Ron Fleming)

started pulling hard again. We just kept putting more distance between us and the Porsche until we ran out of road. I had just won a stoplight Grand Prix against Porsche's finest street offering with only three gears!"

But Doug recalls that he wasn't the one making all the noise: his Porsche-worshipping passenger went berserk. "Bob lost his mind that night. While I had my hands full trying to stay in front of the Porsche, Bob had his eyes forced wide open, and he'd 'seen the light'. Can you give me a hallelujah, Bob? He was transformed. When the poor Turbo owner pulled up next to us at 19th and Newport, Bob was already hanging out the window and heckling the guy so badly that the guy rolled up his window and closed his sunroof, just so he wouldn't have to listen to Bob's mocking!"

But it wasn't only domestic muscle cars or turbocharged Porsches that got dusted off at the lights – even so-called exotica came into Doug Mische's sights whenever the opportunity arose. "One night, while driving home from Auto Haus, where Newport turns into the 55 Freeway, I saw a BMW M1 (yes, a real one) coming up quickly in my rear-view mirror. I put the pedal down and redlined the motor in third, then shifted to fourth and ran it up as far as it would go. The M1 never caught me. I was shocked. So was he, I'll bet, but I could only guess because he stopped racing me once we were really moving. I was having fun – I kept my foot in it

Jeff Kawaguchi's '66 Bug generated a lot of discussion over its Candy Red paintwork and moulded fenders. Some considered it too 'custom' to be a true California Look sedan. Chrome Porsche rims were a throwback to the late-'60s, while Buggy bars weren't popular until the late-'70s. (Dean Kirsten)

until I redlined it in fourth gear. That car was shaking!"

However, your "bad" deeds have a habit of catching up on you, as Doug found out, almost to his cost. "The very next night, I got pulled over by a CHP officer. I had no speedo in the car at that time, just a tachometer and other engine gauges. The officer approached, and asked how fast I was going. He looked inside the car and then asked, 'Where's your speedometer?' I told

him it was out being repaired, but that I thought I was going around 70mph."

"Then came the bombshell: 'How fast do you think you were going last night?' My heart was in my throat. I thought: 'Oh, shit, I'm going to jail.' I played dumb, and he said he had clocked me at 136mph, but he couldn't catch me. I'm guessing the M1 driver had seen the officer and backed out before things got ugly. The officer said to me: 'I don't ever want to see this car

Whatever your feelings about Kawaguchi's car, there's no denying it was a stunning vehicle. It made the front cover of the June 1976 edition of Hot VWs magazine – the second annual California Look issue. (Dean Kirsten)

Compare this view with the Hot VWs *artwork on page 48 and you'll see many similarities. The main differences are the chromed Porsche wheels and the Buggy bars, front and rear. (Dean Kirsten)*

Jeff Kawaguchi had a choice of two engines for his car, a 1968cc "stroker" with dual 48IDAs or a 1700cc "screamer" with dual 40DCN Webers (Dean Kirsten)

going that fast on my road again – is that clear?' Of course, I told him to go screw himself – well, it actually sounded more like 'Yes, sir' when it actually came out of my mouth. But I was amazed that I had gone that fast – and even more amazed and thankful that something hadn't broken."

Jim Edmiston recalls a little fun between friends. "Phil Kelly and I became close neighbours over the years. When we met, Phil was making brake shoes at Raybestos and I was

By the late 1970s, there were changes afoot: Buggy bars, EMPI Spyder Mag wheels and vent windows. California look was evolving… (Dean Kirsten)

working at the Auto Haus warehouse. Phil got the "bug" after a couple of trips in my '63 and I soon hooked him up with a job at Auto Haus. He bought a VW, painted it white like mine and installed an IDA-equipped 1835. One day Phil came by our house to watch a football game. Jim Holmes came by a little later in his white car,

Dave Patrick's Euro-spec Oval-window may have looked like a street car to the casual observer but was a contender in the I/Gas ranks. Its BRM wheels and dechromed, single-colour bodywork all screamed classic California Look. (Dean Kirsten)

In detail, Patrick's car was no show winner – it was built to go fast, nothing more. Running 48IDA Weber carbs on short manifolds was popular 30 years ago but is rarely seen today. (Dean Kirsten)

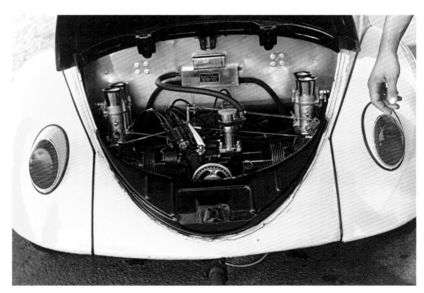

followed by a motorcycle cop who gave him a tongue lashing for accelerating a "little to quickly" for the residential street he was on before letting him go with no ticket. Well, after a few beers, Phil and Jim decided to square off in their cars with me as the starter. We drove over to Lambert Rd and State College Blvd for the big event – unknown to us, a certain cop was sitting in a parking lot nearby and caught the whole show. Turns out, it was the same cop that gave Jim the lecture… We were busted!"

Not every display of horsepower ended happily ever after. Doug Mische had a grandstand view of one of the most famous accidents to have happened at – or, strictly speaking, outside – a Bug-In at Orange County International Raceway. It resulted in an amazing display of camaraderie which has had a lasting effect on Mische. "Looking back on all of this, I guess I hadn't realized that the seemingly few years I had with DKP and my yellow Ghia were among the best times of my life. But not all the times we had were as great. I'm referring to the night that Roger wrecked his Ghia while we were leaving Bug-In 18 in May 1977.

"I've heard from others that the reason Roger lost control of his car is that he had lost his temper talking with the officials at the end of the event, but frankly I don't remember that. I remember leaving, with Roger in the lead

because he was President, and we were doing the usual 'let's make a big exit' thing. Roger had the pedal all the way down and the spot-welded pin on the linkage plates on his 48IDAs had bent – this allowed the accelerator pump cam to go past the pump piston, and it locked his throttles wide open.

"I watched as he did everything he could to stop the car, except turn off the ignition or push in the clutch. The ignition key was on the shifter instead of the dash, and in his panic his hands

Looking at these photos, it's hard to imagine how Roger Grago could possibly have survived this accident. It seems likely that the throttle hung wide open when the linkage went over-centre. With tyres smoking, his Karmann Ghia slammed into a lighting pole outside Orange County International Raceway while leaving Bug-In 18 in 1977. A Herculean effort by fellow DKP club members saw a replacement car built in double-quick time. (Roger Grago)

were firmly gripped onto the steering-wheel, with his elbows locked as he put his full body weight on the brake. With the rear tyres spinning and smoking, and the fronts locked up and smoking, Roger slammed hard into a telephone pole on the access road behind the starting line. His windshield flew out from the force of the impact – his head didn't push it out. That's how hard he hit. His elbows shattered, and his right ankle snapped. The steering-wheel hit him in the

At Bug-In 20, Grago's new Ghia took top honours in the car show. It was a fantastic achievement considering the carnage that had occurred just one year earlier... (Roger Grago)

Mike Martinez's chop-top sedan was the perfect advertisement for his family's bodyshop. With its flawless black paint and detailed Porsche Fuchs wheels, it was beautiful. (Roger Grago)

The car was no slouch, either, thanks to a high-compression stroker motor. The car was ultimately sold to an enthusiast in Japan. (Roger Grago)

chest and caused massive internal injuries. The steering-wheel itself had been bent into a shape that defies description. He had risen so high out of his seat that I could see the back pockets of his Sergio Valentes through the rear window."

It was a massive accident, the outcome of which has remained imprinted on Mische's memory over three decades later. "I don't remember precisely what happened immediately afterwards, because everything was such a blur. Thankfully, those who were better prepared to deal with such events stepped in and took care of Roger, while some of us stood by helplessly wondering what had just happened. Pieces of information filtered through a little at a time, but we really didn't know how bad things were. Everybody seemed to be in shock.

"For something as fun as a Bug-In to change into this nightmare was unimaginable, and it's still very hard to put into words how we felt. The ambulance took Roger to Saddleback Medical Center. Many of us followed. I don't remember who did, and I don't really know if anybody didn't. Once at Saddleback, it transpired that Roger was to be moved to UCI Medical Center in Orange, because Saddleback was not prepared to deal with his extensive injuries. When the ambulance departed, we raced along as near to it as we could without getting arrested or getting in the way. Roger has since said on many occasions that the sound of Weber motors all around him on that trip to hopsital is what

Louis Strahan's mildly-chopped Beetle fought against everything that 1970s California Look stood for, with its flamed paintwork and full bumpers. It proves that not everybody was won over by the Orange County style... (Roger Grago)

Jim Smith's 1967 Beetle represented the best of mid-1970s styling with colour-coded headlamp rims, blacked-out trim and plaid seats. Detailed Porsche Fuchs rims added the finishing touch to this stunning car. (Roger Grago)

kept him going.

"Once we neared UCI Medical, Keith Goss, then owner of one of the most famous chop-top Beetles in VW history, and I (in my Ghia) broke off the 'chase' to go to Al Martinez Paint & Body, where Roger's wrecked car had been taken. Our thinking was that we needed to rescue Roger's 48IDA carburettors before somebody else stole them. Maybe we were idiots for thinking like that, but Keith and I broke into the yard and took Roger's carbs, then tried to get back to the hospital as quickly as we could."

On the way back to the hospital, there was an almost inevitable brush with the law. "We were playing cat and mouse through the streets of Orange County, sliding around corners and driving balls-out, when red lights lit up behind us, and we heard a siren. It seems that one of Santa Ana's finest didn't understand or fully appreciate our urgency. He pulled us both over

and, though I can't remember all the words that were said, we did our best to explain that our good friend had been in an accident and we were merely trying to get to the hospital."

What happened next, despite the gravity of the situation, still brings a smile to Doug's face: "The cop said he was going to have to write us up, anyway, and went to his car to get his ticket book. Maybe, just maybe, he had heard over the radio about the accident out at the track, and took pity on us, because when he got back to Keith and me, he said: 'Well, it looks like this is your lucky night – I'm out of tickets, so I'm letting you go with a warning.'

"I admit that those are most likely not his exact words, but the gist of it is there. He let us off with the 'empty ticket book' excuse. Nice guy. Wish I could send him a Christmas card every year and say thanks. I thought it was quite a moment, and asked if the officer would give us his autograph on the backing of the empty ticket book, but I can't remember whether he did or not. I'm guessing it probably wasn't allowed!"

Mische and his girlfriend, along with Roger Grago's girlfriend, Sheila, and a few more of his friends sat up all night at the hospital, waiting to hear how he was doing. It was a very long night. As Mische says: "It's strange to say 'it was a night I'll never forget', because I only remember parts of it, and most of it is a blur."

The accident, and the events that followed, had a long-lasting effect, not only on Roger Grago, as one might expect, but also on the club. Fellow club member Mike O'Neill donated a Ghia and Mike Martinez got his dad, Al, to provide the paint and bodywork, and everybody else helped put together another Ghia for Grago.

But, as is the case with most clubs, especially those with very young members, one by one members start to focus on different things, like having families and doing different things with their lives and (dare we say it?) growing up. Roger Grago's focus had shifted, and after a period of owning the new Ghia, he decided that he, too, would move on. Doug Mische: "I can't tell you his reasons – all I can tell you is that the club was just not the same once Roger left. He was the glue that kept everybody together. After he went, more guys departed and soon there weren't many of us left.

"The last meeting took place at Cameron Long-

Towards the end of the 1970s, people were trying all kinds of tricks to be different. How about this plaid-covered Karmann Ghia dash? (Roger Grago)

botham's parents' house, and the four remaining members – myself, Ron Greiner, Cameron and Barry Joyce – split what trophies and memorabilia the club had. The hot VW phenomenon seemed to be dying. No matter how urgently those of us who remained wanted to recruit new members and keep DKP alive and strong, the fact was that vans and mini-trucks were in – and muscle cars and hot VWs were out. Two gas crises had all but killed the muscle car, and it somehow became more interesting to young guys to have a slow vehicle you could get laid in than to have a great sleeper like a hot VW."

Mark Thurber was a member of Der Kleiner Panzers, but before that ran with DRF. This rare photograph shows Thurber's car before it was dechromed, or fitted with a Talbot mirror. Thurber was the "T" in FAT Performance. (Ken Jevec)

Chapter 6

YOUNG, FREE & SINGLE IN SoCal

"They handcuffed me, threw me in the back of the squad car and hauled me off to spend the night in jail…"
Dean Kirsten

1970s

I n the late 1960s, there were theoretically numerous vehicle options open to VW journalist Dean Kirsten, who grew up in southern California. Looking back at the used car ads of the time, you could buy a typical big old 1950s Chevy or Ford for just a few hundred bucks or, if you were lucky, persuade your father to sign on the dotted line at the local Mopar dealership and drive away in your new Hemi Challenger… Like I said, if you were lucky.

More realistically, the choice would have been between a few-years-old Ford Falcon or maybe a Chevy II, or Dodge Dart. If you'd been influenced by high-school movies, then a beat-up old sports car from Europe would fit the bill – a Triumph TR3 would have been cool – or perhaps a VW Bus to carry the girls around. But the first choice probably wouldn't have been a 1948 Austin A40 Dorset – unless, of course, it happened to be free. Anything is good if it doesn't eat into the beer budget, right?

Dean – Deano as he is known to all and

Meet the Kirsten family, with Dean Kirsten in the middle. Do you get the impression they might have liked Volkswagens? (Dean Kirsten)

It may not have looked much at the time, but this work-weary '67 had just 60,000 miles on the clock and cost a mere $850. It was the perfect candidate for "The Look" (Dean Kirsten)

After running the it in near stock form, cosmetically-speaking, Kirsten began to start work on the Bug, stripping it of its fenders and bumpers in readiness for a trip to Becker's Bug House for a detrim and repaint. (Dean Kirsten)

sundry – was on the receiving end of just such a vehicular donation, and spent a while rebuilding the engine and getting the sluggish old Brit up and running again. It became his high-school transport in the '60s and fuelled his fascination with oddball drag-racers of the era, as many of the front-running "gassers" in the 1960s were based on British-built Ford Anglias and Austin Devons. Had brotherly influences not taken effect, Deano could easily have spent the rest of his life in the slow lane, at the wheel of some asthmatic Ford…

Late in 1967, Dean's older brother, Eric, decided he wanted to buy a new Volkswagen Beetle. The pair visited their local dealership – Meltebeke VW in La Habra – and were persuaded by the salesman to wait for the "new look" all-new 1968 models which were about to come in. The Kirstens dutifully waited, and looked – and walked away. The heavy "Euro" styling of the '68s just didn't do it for the brothers, leading Eric to search for a good used

The first engine used a 1600cc big-bore kit, along with a Holley Bugspray carburettor, but that made way for this 1835cc unit with dual-port heads and an Engle 110 camshaft. (Dean Kirsten)

The engine was fitted with an S&S exhaust header, with glasspack muffler, and supported by a traction bar. (Dean Kirsten)

example of an earlier model. He eventually purchased a 1963 rag-top sedan, on which Dean honed his mechanical skills, carrying out tune-ups and adjusting the valves.

But after all, this was California in the 1960s, so it was only a matter of time before the modifications began. They fitted a Bosch 031 distributor, re-jetted the carburettor and added a new exhaust system from Phil's Muffler. It was no hot rod, but it was faster than stock – and that was all that mattered. "We used to time the car off the speedo," recalls Deano. "You know, 22mph in first, 35 in second…".

The car continued to be modified further, with Chevrolet rims shod with fatter tyres fitted to the rear. It was fun and typical of the "pre-Cal Look" cars of the era. But it wasn't Dean's. By this time, he'd decided he wanted his own (running) car, so began looking around for a '67 Bug of his own, since a good friend of his owned one and Kirsten "liked the looks and the power". Increasingly, he had seen more and more "finished" fast street VWs – the first of the traditional California Look cars – on the streets around his Fullerton, CA, hunting ground. This was largely due to the number of colleges and high schools in the area, whose students clearly appreciated this new style and enjoyed the performance offered by a well-set-up hot Volkswagen.

Kirsten checked out several cars for sale, among them one example with shaved door handles and, more crucially, no brakes. "I almost crashed it on the test drive! That was a really close call," he recalls. "I decided there and then to build my own car, rather than take on somebody else's abandoned project. Back then there were three major newspapers in the Los Angeles area that had a good assortment of classified ads: the *LA Times*, the *Daily Pilot* and the *Register*. I started looking specifically for '67s, of which there were dozens available – you even had a choice of colour. Sunroof '67 sedans were $800-and-up, with (?) sunroof models being maybe $50 more… I eventually found mine in Long Beach. It was owned by a rather large girl, who wanted just $850 for a car with 60,000 miles on the clock, a repainted nose and a wood stick-on dash, but the rest of it was stock."

Perhaps due to the size of the previous owner, the driver's seat was "toast" and the car had a pronounced lean to the left. But it was solid and priced right, so a deal was struck. On the journey home, Kirsten peeled off the stick-on dashboard covering and tossed it out of the

Once the bodywork and paint had been taken care of, Dean put money aside for a pair of 48IDA Weber carburettors. There was to be no turning back…
(Dean Kirsten)

window. The transformation had begun.

The next day, he decided to rebuild the carburettor, only to drop the easily-dislodged brass accelerator pump nozzle down the intake manifold and into the engine. Things went rapidly downhill from there. A day or two later, he removed the engine and tore it apart, discovering to his horror that the errant pump nozzle had become embedded in the crown of one of the pistons. There was no option but to carry out a full rebuild of the ailing motor.

This called for a trip to the nearby Autohaus parts store, in Buena Park, CA, where he fell under the spell of John Lazenby, one of the founder members of the Der Kleiner Panzers Volkswagen Club. Within a week, the poor unsuspecting '67 had been equipped with an 85.5mm (1600cc) cylinder and piston kit, a Holley Bugspray two-barrel carburettor, S&S extractor exhaust system, lightened flywheel, Bosch 010 centrifugal-advance distributor and a Santana crank pulley. The cylinder heads were also fly-cut by 0.060in to raise the compression ratio. This, Deano refers to as "Stage one"…

Stage two saw him take a trip to Anaheim to see famed customiser George Barris, who installed a Select-A-Drop lowering kit on the front axle beam. The cost? "Drive it in, drive it

out – all for $45!" recalls Kirsten. This would give the car the desirable nose-down California Look rake – no self-respecting hot VW would be seen without it. But the act of dropping the nose of a Beetle automatically placed the headlights below the minimum legal height. Kirsten's route home from college took him along Harbor Boulevard: "The cops would sit by the side of the street and basically ticket every Bug that went past with lowered suspension. I got nailed so many times, it was ridiculous!"

Following one too many tickets, bumpers were refitted to the '67 to keep the local police happy. But T-bars would soon take their place.
(Dean Kirsten)

Virtually every element of what we today think of as "pure" California Look is seen right here: dechromed bodywork, a single straight colour, aluminium T-bars, Lucas turn signals, Talbot mirror, lightweight rims and radial tyres. (Dean Kirsten)

That same weekend, the original bumpers were junked (for the time being, but they would make a return at a later date when the owner fell foul of the so-called "bumper laws") and the stock wheels were treated to a coat or two of gold paint. Inside, the Bug now boasted a Dixco tachometer, Hurst shifter and a Craig 8-track stereo, through which the owner could pump out tunes from favoured bands such as The Who, Grateful Dead, Mothers of Invention, Doors – or just basic surf music from a variety of groups.

Kirsten's worst experience with the Beetle is now a source of amusement, but at the time his

There had always been much discussion about how to install one-piece windows and it was only once Dean Kirsten had sold his car that the problem was solved. Frank's Glass in Bellflower, CA, carried out the conversion to add the finishing touch to this classic Looker. (Dean Kirsten)

Polished DDS "pie-pan" wheels were the defining feature of Kirsten's blue '67. Note, too, the machine-turned Haneline licence-plate frame – a period feature which is rarely seen in modern times (Dean Kirsten)

parents certainly didn't see it the same way – and neither did he. "I'd never had a fix-it ticket with any of my other cars and I got a ticket one time for running without bumpers. I had no idea what to do, so the cop tells me 'You gotta put the bumpers back on and take it along to Fullerton Police department and have the ticket signed off'. So I put the bumpers back on, went to Fullerton where the guy signs off the ticket and said 'OK, that's it'. But what I didn't realise was that I still had to go to court, or at least call to see if there was a fine or something. Of course, I didn't know any better and forgot all about it.

"Six months later, at about 7.00am one

Single quiet-pack muffler was the latest in high-performance exhaust set-ups in the first half of the 1970s. Note that Kirsten decided against filling the cutouts in the rear apron, as well as the holes in the fenders left after removing the US-spec bumpers. (Dean Kirsten)

This photograph taken after the car had been painted by Becker but before a visit to Don Bradford's trim shop. Stock seats and carpet were simply screaming out to be given Brad's magic touch. (Dean Kirsten)

Sunday morning, there's a knock at the door and it was the La Habra Police department with a warrant for my arrest for failing to appear in court. They handcuffed me, threw me in the back of the squad car and hauled me off to spend the night in jail. I had to pay a hundred buck fine to get out, so I guess I'm the only guy around with a criminal record for having no bumpers on a Volkswagen!"

But that brush with the law didn't dampen his enthusiasm. Next in line was a boost in engine output, with the installation of everyone's favourite camshaft, an Engle 110. The cylinder heads were fly-cut still further, this time to 0.120in, the bottom end (crank, flywheel etc) was balanced and a DDS deep sump and traction bar fitted. If Stage three was fun, Stages four, five and six would see things take a turn for the serious when the influence of friend Jim "Sarge" Edmiston came into play.

First of all, the original modified single-port heads were exchanged for a pair of later more-efficient dual-ports, fitted with 40mm inlet valves and matched to polished manifold end-

The dashboard featured S&W gauges set in a panel to the left of the speedometer: ammeter, oil pressure and temperature – but no tachometer. (Dean Kirsten)

Dean Kirsten's "day job" was – and still is – with **Hot VWs** *magazine. Deano can be seen here sitting on the base of the lighting pole at OCIR. (Dean Kirsten)*

Once Don Bradford had worked his magic, the '67 was totally transformed. Blue velour "fat biscuit" inserts with black naugahyde surrounds gave the interior a very classy look. Check out the Haneline machine-turned rocker (sill) and door pillar trims. (Dean Kirsten)

castings. These were then treated to a porting job and used in conjunction with a set of DDS 92mm cylinders and pistons, to give a swept volume of 1835cc. Now it was the turn of the interior. Inside the car, a Motolita steering wheel added some European glamour, while a new DDS shifter replaced the Hurst trigger-style lever.

Up until this point, the car had remained "cosmetically challenged", but the next stage in its development saw it treated to a full strip and repaint in its original VW Blue at Leonard Becker's Bug House in Orange, CA. The bodywork was also fully dechromed at this time. The transformation into what we think of today as a hard-core 1970s Cal Looker continued with the addition of a set of spun-aluminium DDS "pie-pan" wheels, shod with Michelin radial tyres. Designed principally for racing, these light-weight rims gave Deano's car a no-nonsense look that has never gone out of style. The next step was to install a pair of 48IDA Weber carbs, operated by a Berg throttle linkage. Gene Berg also supplied a 1.5in merged exhaust header.

Dean then decided to book the car into Don Bradford's upholstery shop for one of Brad's full-on trademark "fat biscuit" retrims in black naugahyde and blue velour. This beautiful work was augmented by a set of machine-turned Haneline stainless-steel sill covers and, externally, by a pair of aluminium T-bars made by

The stock seats were retained but looked very different with their new trim. Lap-only seat belt was fitted to the driver's side – the passenger had to look after him- or herself... (Dean Kirsten)

A truly classic photo. From right to left: Dean Kirsten's '67, Jim Holmes' white '63 ragtop and Jim Logudice's red '67. Three beautiful cars, each with a style of its own.
(Ron Fleming)

Bug-In 15, October 1975, and under new ownership, the '67 is shown for the first time with one-piece windows. (Dean Kirsten)

friend Mike Leiby. This is what Kirsten refers to as "Stage seven – the DKP phase", as he was approached with regard to membership of this legendary Volkswagen club at about this time in the car's development.

The next chapter in its history – and the last while in Dean Kirsten's hands – came with the installation of a new engine, based around a new crankcase and a set of 88mm (1700cc) Kolbenschmidt cylinders and pistons and new heads prepared by Fleming & Aronson High Performance. It was in this form that the car appeared in the sought-after February 1975 issue of *Hot VWs* as part of the first-ever magazine feature on the California Look. Soon after, the car also became the subject of one of – if not the – first one-piece door window conversions, courtesy of Frank's Glass.

By this time, Dean Kirsten, like many of his peers, was beginning to tire of the street scene and was seduced by the thought of blasting over the sand dunes of Glamis and Dumont in his own sand rail. He swapped the high-compression 1700cc motor for a stocker and sold the sedan to new owner, Julie Martin, for just $1800.

Julie's husband, Mike, continued the car's development by installing his own 1835cc engine, a new headliner and a pair of fresh running boards. At Bug-In 14, held at Orange County International Raceway in April 1975, the Beetle came runner-up in the Semi-Custom class out of 53 entries, proving that it had lost none of its appeal, despite a change of ownership. In fact,

'Saphire (sic) Blues' show card lists all the people who helped with the project. (Dean Kirsten)

as Kirsten recalls, the '67 should have won, as the class-winner was a custom VW Squareback, which had been entered in the wrong class. Had things been different, then there could have been no higher honour than to be a Bug-In champion.

There was one final change made to the car: the installation of one-piece door windows. Dean Kirsten: "One piece windows were one of those subjects that was kicked around for years, but no one could figure out how? Whit Hayden took his car to Becker's and asked the guys there to try and figure out how to install Split-window parts inside the Oval doors, but it never worked. Now, in early 1975, I heard about Frank's Glass in Bellflower, CA, and that he had figured out how to do it. Well, as I sold my car in the February of that year, Mike Martin looked into it and took the car down and had the conversion done, right after getting my car. So, when the '67 was shown next – at Bug-In 15 (October 19, 1975) – it had one-piece windows, and was the first to have them at the Bug-In car show."

In 1976, Mike and Julie Martin sold the car on again, having replaced their engine with a stock

motor, but this time for $2200. The story came to an end a year or so later, when the sedan was stolen and was later reported to have been totalled. It was a sad end to one of the truly classic California Look VWs of all time – a car which has received too little recognition.

Final engine in Dean Kirsten's hands was a high-compression 1679cc motor with an Engle 110 camshaft, dual 48IDAs and a 1.5in Berg exhaust system.
(Dean Kirsten)

When the car was sold in February 1975, the engine was removed and prepared for use in Kirsten's new sandrail.
(Dean Kirsten)

Chapter 7

LIVING LIFE IN THE FAST LANE

"For me, blowing by unsuspecting V8s was, and is, the most fun that you can have without being naked."
Doug Mische

1970s

Back when Doug Mische first saw the light, there were major VW dealerships all over Orange County. Don Burns VW became Garden Grove VW and then finally, when Doug Mische worked there, Mark Howard VW. (Doug Mische)

Doug Mische, by his own admission, is an outspoken individual who seeks the impossible: perfection in all he does. He is a structural engineer with the desire to solve problems which other people don't realise even exist. In short, if something needs to be redone once, twice or three times to satisfy his quest for the best, so be it. His work ethic may not always be shared by those close to him, but it does ensure that whatever Volkswagen he becomes involved with is likely to be the centre of attention, one way or another.

But Doug hasn't always been a VW fan for, back in the 1970s, it was the lure of domestic V8s that he found hard to resist. "The cars I fooled around with back then were all Fords, even though I liked Chevys a lot more," he says

cryptically. "I believe that one of the main reasons I liked Chevys better is that I had worked on Fords – and I owned them because the only cars I could afford just happened to be Fords!

"I had tinkered with a '63 Falcon Sprint, an absolute jewel with bucket seats, a 260ci V8 and a four-speed transmission. This was my first car. Following the Falcon, I bought a '61 Fairlane with a 289 with a tunnel ram and dual Holley carburettors. The car had Plexiglas windows and a 4:11 rear end, and it fooled a lot of people with how much faster it was than it looked. This was the very beginning of my appreciation for 'sleepers'."

Doug's first experience with Volkswagens could have been his last, had he not been open-minded about automobiles in general. "It was in

the spring of 1971 that I had my first experience with VWs, thanks to my first wife, who had bought a 1971 Super Beetle with an Autostick (semi-automatic transmission) when I was in bomb school in the Air Force," he recalls. "It was gutless, yet still fun to drive. But it only impressed me as a fun car, in the same way that the ones Donald Duck drove in cartoons brings a smile to your face."

Fast forward to summer 1974 and Doug had been out of the service only a month or two and was living in an apartment in Orange, CA. The Super Beetle and now ex-wife were long gone, having departed for parts unknown when he received orders to head for Vietnam. Across the hall from his apartment lived a guy named Steve Harlan, who owned a clean yellow Bug, "And," Mische recalls, "when he started it up, the place rumbled! I had never heard a Bug motor make this kind of noise, at least not a street car. I know I must have seen VWs at the drag races, but I guess I was always focused on Funny Cars and rails, and V8s were what I thought made a fast car fast. That changed not long after I met Steve.

"At the time, he had brown triangular decals in his rear quarter windows, with the words "Der Renwagen Fuhrers" written around the edge. I knew nothing of VW clubs and, as most people now know, there wasn't much to know at that time. The original DKP (Der Kleiner Panzers) was long gone and, from the looks of things, DRF was heading that way – it was certainly in its death throes. Still, I got to meet a few other members through Steve, including a very unique guy named Scott Schroeder, and Roger Crawford." Schroeder was to achieve "fame" as the creator of a Bug-In "Worst of Show" winner, as well as a "Best of Show" Karmann Ghia. Crawford became the driver of the *Bad Company* VW drag car, and today is owner of Heads Up Performance, one of the leading VW speed shops in Orange County.

Doug Mische continues: "One day, as Steve and my room-mate Duane and I were sitting around talking cars, Steve began the 'enlightenment'. I remember the smile on Steve's face that day as he listened to first Duane, who owned a '63 Corvette roadster, and me, the 'proud' owner of a less than lightning-fast dead stock '67 Ford Mustang, laughing hysterically as he told us that his VW could outrun either of our cars."

However, tucked away in his garage, Harlan also had an early 1960s Karmann Ghia or, as Mische recalls, "More precisely, what was left of

one. It had started life as a convertible, but the top was long gone. It had a chopped Plexiglas windshield, no interior except for stock seats covered with Royal Tartan seat covers, a custom steering-wheel (a Moto-Lita, I think) and a Plexiglass dash housing some VDO gauges. The decklid was glassfibre, and sported a single cooling grille from a Porsche 356. It had wheels he called 'BRMs', but I had no idea what that meant, and the terms 'Super Diff' and 'close-ratio gears' were too new for me to understand at the time.

"He showed me the car and the motor which, though it looked like a rat's nest, had a very wicked look about it, even to my untrained eyes.

That look says it all: pretty girl and a beautiful car with plenty of horsepower. A hirsute Doug Mische has every right to look happy…
(Doug Mische)

Before the detailed Porsche alloys, the Ghia was equipped with a set of Riviera rims.
(Doug Mische)

It wasn't until the mid-1970s that Karmann Ghias started to gain popularity. Doug Mische's was among the first to appear. (Doug Mische)

Rivieras were never a very popular wheel but had the advantage of being relatively inexpensive and with a favourable offset. (Doug Mische)

A pair of Weber 48 IDA carburettors dominated my view, and I was shocked to think that such a small engine could handle such big carbs. 'Small' – what was I thinking? It was an 82 x 88 (1995cc) motor with an Okrasa crank, ported heads and a merged collector on the exhaust header. I had never seen a VW motor like this, or at least not one that stuck so well in my memory."

Steve Harlan offered his neighbour a ride and Mische, feeling that he owed it to his friend to deflate his opinion of "speed", willingly accepted. "He started the Ghia, and it sounded even more wicked than his sedan had. We drove out of the complex and motored through traffic to the 55 Freeway. It felt pretty bad ass, even though Steve was only giving it moderate throttle," recalls Mische. "We took the on-ramp in second gear, hitting no more than 3000 or 3500rpm, but the second the car was aimed straight, Steve released the monster within.

"He hit full throttle, right at the start of the power band, and took it all the way to the red line: the other cars around us, and the scenery, were already a blur. Then 10 milliseconds later (or so it seemed), he shifted into third and my brain found itself somewhere in the back of my head, with my eyes searching for their openings. We'd just leaped up a whole new level of speed, and were accelerating wildly!"

Doug Mische couldn't believe what was happening! "This is a VW! A cousin to that useless slug my ex-wife drove. How are we moving so damn fast? Seconds later, we hit fourth, but only briefly, as I recall, because we're already going a whole lot faster than everything else and Steve undoubtedly had enough points on his licence that he didn't need to collect any more. We got off the freeway at the next ramp and headed back home. Conversation was useless, because I was dumbfounded, and couldn't hear anything over the noise and vibration the solid-mounted motor and trans were transmitting through the non-insulated interior."

Mische's way of thinking was changed for ever: "My love for 'sleepers' stirred inside me as I

realized I'd just learned a few things about building the ultimate sleeper: a VW! Who would ever have thought?" Within days, he'd traded in his old Mustang for a 1960 Beetle he'd spotted at a used car lot. Big mistake. "I was so emotional about getting a hot VW that I completely overlooked the fact that the car I'd just bought was falling apart so fast it was doubtful it would make it back to the car lot. But it did. I took it back the same day. Ownership of my first VW had lasted less than four hours!"

A few months later, Mische landed a job with the US Post Office and, compared to his previous employment, it was big money. He was now in a position to buy his neighbour's car.

"Steve had kept the drivetrain and the BRMs, but all I needed to do was build my own motor and trans and get my own BRMs. It never happened. I never touched that car until the day I sold it. The job only lasted three months, and the money tree died with it. I sold the Ghia to Jim Gay, at Wrecks West, and never saw it again," Mische wistfully remembers. "I hadn't had the chance to build my own VW yet, but the desire to build one was now inside me for ever."

It was around this time that Doug's old Ford Mustang started dying. The engine block was cracked and the auto transmission was slipping badly, so it was time to look for another car. "I went to Don Burns in Garden Grove (a well-

Mische's Ghia was probably one of the best-looking ever built. Its blacked-out trim and Fuchs alloys gave it a Porsche-like character. (Doug Mische)

Viewed side-on, the car sat 'just right' with a hint of nose-down rake. "Caramel" paint added to the low-key character. (Doug Mische)

known VW dealership) and found a 1969 Karmann Ghia that was pristine, except for a small dent in the deck lid. I guess it hadn't been on the lot long enough to get the bodywork done. I was young and dumb at that time, and never thought to haggle over the price, but that first ride in Harlan's Ghia was seriously clouding my judgment and I had to have this car. It was Oriole Yellow with a brown interior, a coupé, and it was fantastic. I think they wanted $2495 for it then, which was probably what the last new ones had cost. But Ghias had disappeared from the VW sales floors by then. It was 1975 and the last Ghia had rolled off the line over a year ago. So I paid the asking price and headed home…"

Shortly after buying the Ghia, Doug Mische had the good fortune to get a job at Auto Haus, the leading VW aftermarket specialist in Southern California, with a string of shops across Orange County. This gave him the chance to buy all the parts he wanted at a discount. "The first stint at Auto Haus wasn't a happy time. John Lazenby was the general manager, and he was serious about the way that store – and all the stores – ran. I was a goofball long-haired kid with a huge chip on my shoulder, and John and I butted heads. It was not a good career move on my part.

"Within a year I was gone, and then I got hired by Roger Crawford's older brother, John, who had a shop in Costa Mesa (Crawford Engineering). He had been a customer at Auto Haus, and offered me a job building VWs." Mische jumped at the chance but, as he admits, "Poor John didn't know what he was getting. I knew practically nothing about VWs, and my irritating ability to take too long to do things just right was already in full swing. Within three months John had let me go, because there was no way he could make money with me!

"I had a hard time finding a job after that, and finally landed a parts counter job with a local motorcycle shop that sold Honda, Yamaha and Triumph motorcycles. It was money, and I earned enough to start putting some pieces on the Ghia. First of all I got a header system, some Riviera wheels and some suspension pieces so that the car at least looked like it was fast. I loved what I had seen on Cal Look Bugs while working at Auto Haus, and thought the Ghia would look good with the same treatment."

Mische dechromed the car, but not by removing the trim. Instead, he chose to paint it, as he thought that shape would look better with the double side trim than if it were removed. "I painted everything that was chrome, black. I had never heard of powder-coating (I'm not sure if it even existed then) and my technique to get paint to stick involved roughing the surface lightly, painting it with high-heat satin black paint, then baking it in the oven. Julie, my girlfriend of six years, must have loved that! After it came out, I rubbed some Armor-All on it and put the trim back in the oven. It worked OK and it lasted better than anodizing, which always seemed to turn purple after some time in the sun."

The clean lines of Mische's Ghia didn't go unnoticed: "One day, a guy pulled up in an early sedan with a rag-top sunroof. The car was very

Fitting 7Jx15 Porsche alloys to the rear completely changed the look of the Ghia. Blacked-out headlamp rims and turn signals were subtle touches which helped achieve the "stealth" look Mische was seeking. (Doug Mische)

With the tachometer from a Porsche 911 and a full set of VDO Cockpit gauges, the crackle-finish dashboard of Mische's Ghia would have looked at home in a race car. Shifter was by DDS. Note the centre-cap from a Porsche alloy used as a horn push. (Doug Mische)

clean, with unique wheels and Buggy bumpers. It sounded really good. Turns out he'd been taking Newport Boulevard to and from work, and had seen the Ghia parked out on the street. His name was Randy Welch and he was one of the three founders of the second generation of DKP." But the significance of that piece of information was lost on Doug at the time.

"He asked if I'd like to join his club. Back then, I had no knowledge of DKP, so I didn't know what honour was being offered to me. He said the car looked good, and explained that all the cars in the club had motors that weren't stock. My heart sank when he asked what I had in the Ghia – it was bone stock except for the header, and maybe an 010 distributor. It even still had the original single-port heads!"

Welch suggested that Doug Mische attend a meeting, anyway, which he did. He admits to being stunned when he saw all the exceptionally clean cars the members were driving. "I thought to myself: 'My wreck does not belong here,' but I wasn't going to say it first. After getting to know the guys and their cars, I decided I really wanted to be a part of this. After the required three consecutive meetings, the guys voted on whether I should be accepted into the club and, to my shock and amazement, I was."

There were, however, a couple of conditions:

he had to fix a couple of dings in the body, and he had to try to build a motor as soon as he could! "Ha!", exclaims Mische, "Like just hearing their motors wasn't already enough incentive. I cannot describe how small a guy can feel showing up at a DKP meeting with the only motor that sounds like a three-legged wheezing gerbil on a treadmill as the sole source of power. I promised. And I delivered... sorta."

A few weeks after Mische became involved

A pair of Huntmaster seats replaced the originals, helping to hold the driver and passenger in place. They were later swapped for a pair of Recaros once Doug started working at Chick Iverson Porsche. (Doug Mische)

The 2160cc motor ran IDAs on short manifolds, with a Scat 84mm crank, H-beam rods, Engle 130 cam and 90.5mm cylinders. Heads were by Stu Thomas, with 44 x 37.5mm valves. Note the polished stainless firewall. (Doug Mische)

Auto Haus Costa Mesa, circa 1977–78. The Auto Haus chain of stores was the number one source of aftermarket parts for VWs. Doug Nadasdy in the triped shirt was known as "Doug Bug" while Doug Mische was known as "Doug Ghia"… (Doug Mische)

with DKP, *Dune Buggies & Hot VWs* magazine hosted a navigational "poker run"-style rally called the California 1000, and it was a two-day event that supposedly covered 1000km. "At the start of the rally, a photographer approached me and said: 'I'd like to do an article on your Ghia. It's the first Cal Look one I've ever seen.' If I hadn't been sitting, I'd have fallen over! At first I

thought the guy had been on earth for maybe only a week and had never seen Roger Grago's car. And I can only assume that his definition of Cal Look was more along the lines of dechromed and de-bumpered, because Roger's car was gorgeous and seemingly perfect to me… except for the chrome and the bumpers."

With the sheer panic of getting a motor built before *DB&HVW*s got tired of waiting, and the promise he'd made to DKP, Mische set out to buy parts – and fast. "I had been rehired by Auto Haus under very sad conditions, a counterman I had come to know and like was in a motorcycle accident on Christmas Eve and, after a week-long coma, he died. Auto Haus needed someone with experience to replace him, and they called me in. I had very little money with which to buy any engine parts, and could not afford a new engine case, so bought the case that was used in the Auto Haus display motor for $25! This would later prove to be a disastrous decision, but it did allow me to build a motor for the Ghia without having to have my daily (only!) driver off the road while I built an engine."

Mische bought a pair of dual-port heads, NPR 87mm pistons and cylinders, an Engle 120 cam and a used pair of 42DCNFs with which to assemble his first "hot" motor. "Yes, my first "built" motor was an over-cammed 1641 with stock heads, a non-counterweighted stock crank and a junk engine case!" laughs Mische. "I contacted *Hot VWs* and told them I was ready.

Anyone who has seen the 'Caramel Ghia' article in that *Hot VWs* magazine knows how far from ready I was. The rear fenders had holes from where the bumper had been bolted, I had a parking sticker covering the dent in the decklid, and I had done virtually no engine detailing. But I was in a magazine! And I had a hot motor! Yeah, man! It was great. It did at least prove that you could jet Webers to run smoothly on a very small motor, even with stock heads."

Like most young enthusiasts, the prospect of having his car featured in a national magazine was a real high point in Mische's life. "But I hadn't built the motor myself. At the time, it seemed like black magic to me, and I enlisted the help of a guy named Scott, who owned the silliest named automotive repair shop I'd ever heard of: Datsa Toyota Volksa Porsche. It was a ridiculous name, but clearly it was also memorable. Scott was a regular customer of Auto Haus, and he 'volunteered' his services following unrelenting pressure from me to show me what was involved. After seeing it done, I felt ridiculous, but it felt as if the secrets of the universe had just been revealed and I would soon be building my own."

Like so many people who've never experienced life with a modified Volkswagen, Doug Mische was astounded by the increase in performance. "I was absolutely amazed at what a difference a few horsepower made. I had no idea how much horsepower that badly mismatched little motor made, but I'm willing to bet it couldn't be more than 70 or 80bhp. Yet driving the Ghia was so much more fun, and almost immediately I started lusting for a bigger mill. And I wouldn't have to wait long…

"One day, after getting to work, I found the engine leaking very badly, and discovered that I had cracked that cheap engine case right across the top. My first engine was done. But, since working at Auto Haus paid better than selling parts at a motorcycle shop, I'd been able to start collecting pieces and found I could afford to build a motor right. I had won a Berg counter-weighted 69mm crank at a rally, I bought some Mahle 88mm pistons and cylinders, and also a set of ported 40mm x 35.5mm cylinder heads from Stu Thomas at Headflow Performance. Stu

and I had worked together at Crawford Engineering, along with Bruce Simurda (now editor of *Hot VWs* magazine), but Stu had left to start his own head-porting shop. In my opinion, Stu was an excellent head porter, not one of the best known, but his work was very good and his heads really flowed. The new 1700 was a much better match for the 120 cam, and some 48IDAs responded even better. That engine ran great – many people were surprised to discover they'd been outrun by just a 1700."

But Mische wanted still more horsepower! "Who doesn't? The other guys in the club had faster cars and bigger motors, and I wanted to run with the big dogs. Roger Grago had a 1776, as did Mike O'Neill, and Mike's motor had Fumio heads, an Engle 140 and tons of compression. That car had run in the high 12s with a 1776! My friend Ron Greiner had something over two-litres – I think it was a 2074 – and he always wanted to bump Mike off the DKP Top 10 board. I remember a few wild races between the two of them in front of our Fullerton clubhouse after meetings.

"I bought engine parts like other people buy groceries. In fact, that's the money I used. If you see early pics of me, you'll see the effects!" laughs Mische. "I'd pay the rent, the utilities and the car payment, then buy a stack of chicken pot-pies to keep me alive, while every spare nickel went into parts. I had bought a new German engine case (I'd learned that lesson well enough) when I built the 1700 and I hadn't put many miles on it, and it was already bored for 88s so there was no reason to replace it already.

Doug Mische reckons he bought engine parts like other people bought groceries in the search for reliable horsepower. The Ghia ran a variety of engines, ranging from a 1641 with 42DCNF Webers, which Mische hated, all the way up to the high-compression IDA-equipped 2160cc unit shown opposite. (Doug Mische)

Mische reckons that the time he spent with fellow Der Kleiner Panzer club members were among the happiest in his life. (Doug Mische)

"I bought a 78mm crank from Gene Berg, and an Engle 130 cam from work, and my second set of heads from Stu Thomas, with welded ports and 42mm x 37.5mm valves. I never dyno'd my motors, but this little 1900 really ran. Though the Ghia was heavy, it was still fairly fast, and I had at last acquired enough horsepower to get on the DKP Top 10 board myself. Although there were guys running around in those days with faster VWs, I still had plenty of fun surprising the muscle car guys with this little VW.

"I remember coming down Newport Boulevard on the way to work one morning, and a guy with an early '70s Chevy Nova was about to turn onto the street. I noticed he had a tunnel ram with dual Holley carburettors sticking out of the hood, but I got the impression that the car had little else. He came out onto Newport, nailed it and so did I – all he saw were my taillights getting smaller. I smoked this guy! He was stunned. Like most guys with enough ego to put such a ridiculous induction system on a street car, he didn't want to talk about what had just happened, and turned at the next street. For me, blowing by unsuspecting V8s was, and is, the most fun that you can have without being naked."

Now Doug Mische was – and still is – as we have already established, not backwards about coming forwards, to use an old expression. He was also trying his best to be law-abiding… maybe. "I felt I needed to honour the law's desire for me to keep my speed down, so I bought close-ratio gears and a Super-Diff for my gearbox. Now the little beast accelerated even faster on the top end! I was having a blast. My car was never *the* fastest in DKP, but it was *one* of the fastest, and it seemed appropriate to let everybody know I thought so. I was so modest!

"I got a licence plate that read FASRNU, and now it seemed pretty easy to find people to race. Everybody and their brother who saw that plate wanted to blow my doors off, but only one car ever beat me. I chose my races carefully (well, as carefully as street racing allows) and never went up against something that I knew would smoke me. The car that did beat me was a beautiful yellow Z28 Camaro. We were stopped at a freeway off-ramp, and I threw this guy a rev – and when he threw one back, I knew I'd screwed up. You could hear the blower whine as the revs came down. The guy was running an under-the-hood supercharger and, judging by how little time I had to look at the disappearing Chevy's rear end, it was overdriven pretty good!" Oh well, nobody's perfect.

Although he spent most of his time trying to make the Ghia quicker than the car in the next lane, Mische also did his best to make the show match the go. "The club wanted every car to look like it could enter a car show at the drop of a hat and, as I look back, I think most of them did. Personally, I wanted my Ghia to look as good – or better – than Roger Grago's, but I could never quite get to that point because I threw almost all of my money at the motor. But I did my best to make the engine and interior look trick.

"I must have tried four or five different dashboard configurations while I owned the car, one being aluminium with black wrinkle finish that Auto Haus sold, another in polished brass (what a pain that was!) and a third covered with fabric that sort of matched the interior colour. But I never had the resources to get the car perfect. Roger's Ghia, and most other cars in the club, had interiors that were done by Brad's, and the seats matched the door panels and the carpet looked new.

"I had some Huntmaster seats in the car for a while, because the stock buckets didn't feel the way I wanted the car to feel. After leaving Auto Haus in 1978, I went to work for Chick Iverson VW Porsche Audi and started making really good money. I bought a pair of Recaro LS seats – those seats were the best! OK, so the fabric didn't match my interior colour very well, but everybody that sat in them didn't seem to mind."

The search for perfection didn't end there,

either. "I had a variety of wheels on the car, too. I started with a set of Rivieras, then I traded a Bultaco Pursang motorcycle for a set of 6Jx15 Porsche alloys. I tried polished 14-inch EMPI eight-spokes for a while, too, but I really liked the alloys better, and settled on another set of what were 5.5Jx14 on the front and 7Jx15 at the rear. I remember how much interest there was in those seven-inch rears at the first rally I went to with them on the car. Nobody could believe that I'd squeezed them under the stock fenders, which weren't all that stock by the time I'd got done grinding and pounding on the body to make the tyres clear! But I loved the look! My favourite picture of the car is one of it doing a burnout at Bug-In, and those wheels can be clearly seen in the photo."

Mische was always hard on transmissions. Racing a motorcycle one night, he found himself heading for a set of railroad tracks flat out in third gear. "As I drove over the tracks, there was a huge bang and the engine over-revved. Race over, the Honda went by and I searched for a gear. It went right back into third, and drove perfectly, but when I got home, as I stepped out of the car I almost broke my back slipping on the floor. There was a growing puddle of gear oil

under the car and a trail leading up the driveway.

I looked underneath to find gear lube was pouring out of the front of the transmission. Then I saw what had happened: the trans had hit one of the tracks right under the ring and pinion – it had hit so hard that the nose-cone broke in two, allowing the casing to stretch and pull the trans

Mische's Ghia as part of the DKP club display at a Bug-In. (Doug Mische)

His favourite photo of the car shows it on the startline at OCIR. (Doug Mische)

The Ghia was always on borrowed time as, in common with many VWs back then, it was eventually stolen, stripped and burnt out. A sad end to a great car. (Doug Mische)

FAT Performance made a dual quiet-pack exhaust system to replace the Auto Haus set-up previously used. Note the "FASRNU" plate. (Doug Mische)

out of gear!"

Sometimes Doug wasn't quite so lucky with transmission breakages. "One night, leaving the meeting, I smoked the tyres, jerked second gear and found I was still in first. Shifter in second, trans in first, and it didn't want to shift. Uh-oh. So here I was, stuck in first gear and more than 20 miles from home. Should I be smart and call a flat-bed tow truck? Hell, no – I'm an idiot. Let's just drive it; how bad can it be? Redline in first, coast, redline first, coast… repeat ad infinitum. I think it took two hours!

"When the trans came out, I found it had a broken shift fork. Why? Because I had left the stock brass one in there. So that meant another trip to see the late Hap Ponce… Hap and I had

worked together at Mark Howard VW in Garden Grove (it had started life as Don Burns VW, then became Garden Grove VW and finally Mark Howard bought it). Hap and Terry Mish (no relation!) had a Type 3 Fastback race car called *Mishap*, a clever use of both their names.

"Hap was great at building gearboxes and I sure gave him plenty of practice! Before Hap came along, Bill Taylor had done my trans work, but I lost contact with him when I left Chick Iverson. I don't remember who fixed or installed what, but both of them got a chance to do a lot of work for me.

"But whoever had installed my close-ratio third and fourth gears hadn't installed a hardened key on third, and so that was another thing that failed one night. If you've never sheared a third-gear key, it's something that you have to experience to fully appreciate.

"In my case, third gear would still work unless you put too much power to it. Then it would make noises like you had tried to save money by using gravel as a lubricant rather then gear lube. It was a horrendous sound and feeling: it's like every part in the box is trying to re-enact 'The Great Escape'!

"The 2160cc motor that was in the Ghia at that time was the last one I built for it. I had bought some of the best pieces that were around at the time. It had a Scat 84mm forged crank, chrome-moly H-Beam rods, thin-wall wrist pins, 90.5mm pistons and cylinders and a 10.5lb flywheel. I used a brand-new engine case and had Stu Thomas make me one last pair of heads. They were 44mm x 37.5mm welded dual-ports, and the intakes were welded on the roofs and floors, and the ports moved further apart so the path to the inlet valve was as straight as possible.

"These heads were beautiful, and they flowed a ton. Maybe not compared to some of the heads around today, but for back then they were pretty special. And they cost $1200 in the late 1970s, a huge amount of money at the time. I don't remember what they flowed or what compression the motor ran, but I think it was around 11:1 or 11.5:1. I kept the Engle 130 cam from before, and put on a 1.625-inch merged collector exhaust. I also had FAT Performance make a custom set of dual mufflers that looked much better than the Auto Haus version. It was never dyno'd, so there's no way to know the horsepower, but it ran like an ape with its ass on fire!"

When the club scene started to wind down in the late 1970s, life with the Ghia took one more

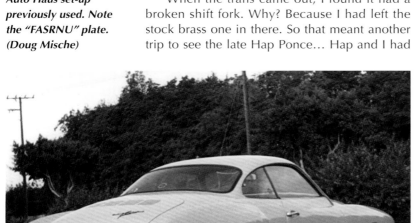

Doug Mische was overjoyed to be reunited with his "lost" Karmann Ghia in 2008. Despite rumours to the contrary, the car had not been burnt following its theft in the 1970s, but had been rebuilt. Following up on a lead, Mische was eventually able to buy back his old car. (Author)

wicked turn. Doug Mische had met a charming young girl called Kathy while working at Commonwealth VW in Santa Ana, housed in a converted supermarket on Bristol Street. "This dealership was unique in that the parts department and service bays were separated by a wall that didn't go to the ceiling so, as the mechanics worked on Beetles and Buses, we all happily breathed carbon monoxide and watched the soot settle on all the parts. If you bought parts at this location, you can rest assured you bought some of the dirtiest new VW parts ever sold! We went home as black as any of the mechanics every day!

"Kathy had come in to buy a new emergency brake handle for her Karmann Ghia, because the button had popped out and hit the dashboard. I fixed it for her instead of taking her money, and told her to have her brakes adjusted so it wouldn't happen again. Apparently, I made an impression. A week or so later, I took a new job at Jim Marino VW in Huntington Beach, and when Kathy came in one day looking for me, I asked her out.

"We went to a movie in Orange, a matinée. She loved Karmann Ghias and was having a ball riding in mine. I told her how fast it was and, of course, she didn't believe me. That so reminded me of myself and the ride in Steve Harlans' Ghia, so I punched it a few times and she thought it was pretty bitchin'. We were having a very good time, until we came out of the movies – and where my car had been parked was a very different car, and some broken glass on the ground. The reality sank in – my beloved Ghia was gone, and it was gone for good."

Mische was eventually contacted by the LA Sheriff's Department and told that his car had been found in Compton, but it had been stripped and burned. The motor, the transmission, the Porsche wheels and gauges, the Recaro seats, an original DKP hood badge and his beloved FASRNU licence plate were all gone. And he had no insurance.

"Trying to replace that car wasn't possible," Mische recalls. "I owned a lot of different cars, but I couldn't bring myself to do it all over again. Thankfully, I hadn't had it stolen while Der Kleiner Panzers was together as a club. At least I had been able to cruise with some of the best guys I've ever known, in a car that was unbelievably fun to drive and faster than a lot of unsuspecting drivers thought. I had owned the car for only six or so years, but it provided me with a lifetime of memories. It played a big part in my finding the longest-lasting and best friendships I never dreamed of having."

Chapter 8
IT'S PARTY TIME!

"My first thought was: 'How long am I going to be in jail for this?' I pulled right over and waited..."

1980s

Formed in the latter part of the 1970s, DKK acheived notoriety in the 1980s, with the Bug-In events becoming a major club focus.

With the burgeoning club scene heading into steady decline towards the end of the 1970s, things didn't look too promising for the future of the California Look. Even the enthusiast VW press seemed to lack any real conviction, featuring cars which were more "custom" in finish than the traditional Lookers of old. Maybe it was the increasing price of gas, or the ever-more complex smog laws that were putting people off, but it began to seem as if the days of the hot-rod Volkswagen were numbered. Or were they?

In fact, if you look at attendance figures for events such as the Bug-In, more people attended the shows in the last two or three years than had been the case in the 1970s, when conventional wisdom suggests the scene was at its zenith. Magazine circulation figures were on the increase, too, but the cars the magazines featured were changing – and that was a sure sign that the owners were as well. The old guard had stepped aside to make way for a new, younger generation, one which had a more carefree outlook on life as a whole. The Vietnam War was long over and the shadow of the draft was no longer hanging over young men in their teens and early twenties. The 1980s were a time to have fun, with few responsibilities!

Musically, there were major changes afoot – the music television station MTV was launched

Bob Scicareos' Nuthin' Fancy was typical of many show cars of the 1980s. But despite its Candy paintwork and polished Porsche alloys, it still retained the vital elements of the classic California Look. (Greg Brinton)

in 1981, heralding the arrival of the pop video as an art form in its own right. Michael Jackson's 'Thriller' album was released in 1982, as was the first single by a female vocalist called Madonna. Other bands went on to become household names in the 1980s, such as Dire Straits, Van Halen, Duran Duran, U2 and The Police, to name but a few. While many music fans brought up on a diet of The Rolling Stones, The Who and The Beatles might have looked down their noses at this new generation of super-group, there was no getting away from the fact that, for the most part, they were here to stay.

New VW clubs began to form, some with less stringent membership requirements than, say, Der Kleiner Panzers or Der Renwagen Fuhrers. One of the best known was DKK – Der Kleiner Kampfwagens – an Orange County-based club which had formed back around 1977, but achieved widest recognition in the early 1980s, as it was one of the biggest to have survived the Cal Look "depression". Many of the cars that grew out of the 1980s, although still termed "Cal Lookers" by magazines, bore little resemblance to cars like Greg Aronson's seminal '63 rag-top. Pastel colours and colour-coded headlamp rims

(and even bumpers) started to appear under the "Cal Look" label, much to the chagrin of die-hard enthusiasts.

Indeed, although membership of DKK was dependent on ownership of a finely-detailed VW, some cars with a more "custom" flavour were welcomed, too. As a consequence, a few

Classic style: nose-down and dechromed.
(Glenn Gaskey)

Giving your car a name was popular in the '80s.
(Greg Brinton)

Nuthin' Fancy may have looked like a show car but it was built to deliver! 2276cc engine featured Superflo heads by Dave Kawell, dual 48IDAs and nitrous oxide injection – a potent combination. (Greg Brinton)

Scicareos' car was detailed throughout. In the trunk, alongside the velour-covered spare wheel, lay a custom-painted nitrous oxide bottle, labelled "secret sauce". This helped make the car almost unbeatable in street races. (Greg Brinton)

of the club cars sported lowered suspension, both front and rear (although not to the extremes of the Resto-Cal movement of the 1990s and beyond), colour-coded brightwork and graphics. Yes, multi-hued "graphic" paintjobs started to appear on what were still being referred to as California Look sedans, with bold striping along the lower body and occasionally over the roof, too, becoming popular in some quarters. It was at total odds with the no-frills minimalism of 1970s California Look, but it is not difficult to understand why this change in style came about. After all, 1980s culture was very different to that of the '70s, and there was a feeling in some quarters that it was time for something new.

DKK's Bill Schwimmer (later a founder-member of the third generation of DKP) is quoted in an interview by Stephan Szantai in *Ultra VW* magazine as saying: "The pastel-coloured cars evolved from the desire to be different. There were so many black, tan, red or blue cars in those days…" Schwimmer, whose cars are detailed in the following chapter, himself first drove a red 1970 Beetle, followed by a red Squareback, which was then finally redone in a shade of pink. The cars were not what one would today think of as Cal Look, but they were very representative of the scene in the early 1980s.

The dashboard was little changed from stock, with the exception of a range of VDO Cockpit gauges to the left of the speedometer and a tach slung from a bracket below the ashtray. Shifter was by Berg. (Glenn Gaskey)

As Stephan Szantai was keen to point out, Der Kleiner Kampfwagens' influence spread throughout the scene over a period of many years. It is one of the club's members, Henry Mayeda, for example, who is credited with starting what is today referred to as the "Old School" style of California Look. Mayeda's take on things was to drive a 1967 Beetle with full trim and bumpers, yet with a dual Weber-carbed motor and BRM wheels. This style was completely at odds with the traditional California Look, with its almost total lack of body mouldings and bumpers.

Even though the pastel paintwork, graphics and full trim all paint a picture of a purist style in decline, the truth is actually very different. The Look was simply evolving for, at the heart of it all, there was still a desire to own, build and drive a high-powered Volkswagen capable of eating alive V8 muscle cars. Engines varied in size from 1776 "big-bore" motors up to 2180cc (or more) "strokers", almost always fitted with the ubiquitous 48IDA Weber carburettors. That at least continued a tradition which started back in the very early 1970s…

A fine example of one of the new-wave Cal Lookers was Bobby Scicareos' *Nuthin' Fancy* 1967 sedan, which was put together with the help of his friend, and current DKP member,

Glenn Gaskey. Gaskey recalls that the car was in pretty decent shape when offered for sale by Dyno Don Chamberlin, and not what you'd call "resto material". Scicareos liked fast, low, clean cars, so the Bug was built in stages. Stage one was to lower the suspension, fit a set of alloys (Porsche Fuchs rims were, and still are, almost universally referred to simply as "alloys" within the scene) and then spray it in purple primer.

The next step was to install a big motor – in this case, a 2276cc engine with an 82mm

VW Seat Covers in Garden Grove was responsible for the velour trim. Note the one-piece door window glass – a very popular feature by the 1980s. (Greg Brinton)

Glenn Gaskey didn't set out to have a pink (or should that be 'Porsche Raspberry'?) Karmann Ghia, but the painter – Randy Schwimmer, brother of fellow DKK member, Bill – had other ideas. Clearly the end result appealed to the girls…
(Glenn Gaskey)

Polished rims from a Porsche 914 replaced the Riviera wheels with which the Ghia was originally equipped. Colour-coded headlamp rims and fresh-air grilles, along with smooth bumper blades, helped give the car a very stylish appearance.
(Glenn Gaskey)

stroker crank and Carrillo rods, 94mm pistons and cylinders, Kawell-prepared SuperFlo heads cut for 9.5:1 compression, dual 48IDA Webers and, as the crowning glory, nitrous oxide injection. This potent combination was used in conjunction with a Don Strong-built transmission with close-ratio gears and a Super-Diff heavy-duty differential. This was followed soon after by stage three, which saw the car equipped with disc brakes, safety harnesses, a line-lock and new sports seats.

It was in this form that Glenn Gaskey drove it

in a number of street races, where its innocuous purple primer, allied to its breathtaking performance, won it the nickname "Purple People Eater". Such was its reputation that, as Gaskey remembers all too well, after a while nobody would take on the challenge – it was time to move on to stage four.

This saw the car torn apart and repainted in a beautiful Candy Burgundy, overlaid with purple pearlescent lacquer. The inscription "Nuthin' Fancy" was airbrushed across the decklid at the same time. The interior was retrimmed, too, with grey velour seats, door panels and trunk, all by VW Seat Covers in Garden Grove. The finishing touch was a colour-coded nitrous oxide bottle in the trunk, bearing the legend "Secret Sauce". Glenn Gaskey recalls how the car was "street driven – hard! Bobby raced everything! The car stayed at my mother's house and Bobby would get through 20lbs of nitrous every week!" Eventually, it was sold to make way for an even faster '67…

Glenn Gaskey's own first VW was a real child of the new decade. Purchased in 1980, his 1969 Karmann Ghia still wore its original Burnt Orange paint and a set of Riviera wheels, and ran a 1641 motor with dual Kadron carburettors. The first thing that went through Gaskey's mind was to have the car repainted. "Bill Schwimmer's brother, Randy, was a painter. He

had the bodywork all prepped and told me to come down and take a look at the colour he had chosen. It turned out to be Porsche Raspberry! I said 'No way!', to which he replied, 'OK, get it out of here, then…'. I succumbed and it was painted a fetching shade of pink."

While he was reassembling the car, Glenn took the opportunity to make some changes. Inside, he replaced the stock trim panels with sheet aluminium, which was painted pink – sorry, Porsche Raspberry – to match the body-work. To his way of thinking it made the interior look huge! A set of detailed Porsche 914 2.0-litre alloys was also fitted in place of the Rivieras. The "little" engine had to go, too. This made way for a 76mm x 90.5mm (1955cc) combination with heads by Dave Kawell in Santa Ana and dual 40IDF Webers, along with a Don Strong-built trans with close-ratio third and fourth gears. Although it sounded a mild set-up, once the carburettors were upgraded to 48IDAs and a merged exhaust header fitted, the Ghia ran 13.70–13.80-second quarter-mile times. Finally, a Britax sunroof and a pair of Corbeau sports seats completed the project.

The car may have been conspicuous in its pink paint, but that didn't stop Glenn Gaskey and friends creating a little havoc in it. "I was on the way to Camelot – a popular cruising spot in Anaheim – one night with my friend Dave

Mason in the Ghia. I was trying to make a left turn onto La Palma Avenue, just as the traffic signal was changing, but the car oversteered hard, bringing the back end all the way round. As I slid my way across the intersection, an Anaheim motorcycle cop was heading east on La Palma and saw me spin out in front of him. In an effort to avoid hitting me, he laid his bike down on its side!

"I watched him out of the side window of my car as he dropped his bike, and the first thing that went through my head was: 'How long am I going to go to jail for this?' I pulled over and waited as he picked up his motorcycle, walked over to the curb and approached the Ghia. He

Lowered front and rear suspension always looks good on a Ghia, just so long as there is still that "hot-rod" rake…
(Glenn Gaskey)

Aluminium dash panel with VDO gauges reflects the pink paint used on the door panels.
(Glenn Gaskey)

1955cc engine originally relied on dual 40IDF Webers, but these were later upgraded to 48IDAs. Note polished aluminium firewall. (Glenn Gaskey)

A common sight today, the Autometer "Monster" tach chosen by Gaskey for his Cabriolet may well have been the first ever fitted to a VW. (Glenn Gaskey)

subject of a basic restoration, with new paint, top, interior, brakes and an 1835cc motor with a single Zenith carburettor. It still sat at the stock ride height on a set of chromed steel rims. "Fortunately, when I sold the Ghia, I'd kept the motor and a freshly-built Don Strong transmission, both of which immediately went into the Cabriolet," recalls Gaskey. "I also fitted a set of red and white stock wheels and then added an AutoMeter Monster tach under the dashboard. As far as I know, this was the first time I'd seen one in a VW." In this guise, the car ran mid-13-second quarter-mile times and saw a lot of street race action, especially on the infamous Whittier Boulevard, in Los Angeles.

"This was a real party car!" says Glenn Gaskey. "We'd take out the passenger seat and Greg Brinton, myself and some other hooligans would put a keg of beer on the floor and drive around tempting fate – although we never got caught." Soon after, the engine was further updated with an 82mm SPG roller-bearing crank and a pair of Drino Miller cylinder heads. Fast just became faster…

"One night on West Street, right next to Disneyland, I pulled up next to my friend Frank Fabozzi (see page 135) in his raspberry '56 sedan. We were sat under the monorail crossing at a red light, so my buddy jumped out of my car and flag started us right there! What we didn't know, though, was that there was an Anaheim Police Department patrol car sat behind the bushes at the intersection…

"Well, the light turned green and we got flagged off, and away we went. I had Frank covered until I shifted into third, at which point the transmission went 'boom!' – I'd broken third gear! Frank took off and I turned into a driveway. I managed to talk my way out of trouble as it was such a stock-looking car. I argued that how could I possibly race with no third gear in a stock convertible Bug? It must have been the other guy making all the noise!'

Having mischievous fun was very much the DKK way, and it didn't always directly involve cars, as demonstrated by Scott "Worm" Blaydes' tale of life in the club in general, and memories of Bug-In 27 in particular. "Our club was once again the most represented club at this, the holiest of VW events. Over the previous few years, our cars had won Best of Show, Best Squareback, Best Interior, and more. We were turning away new members whose cars were not up to our idea of perfection, recruiting only the

then opened the door, pulled me out by my collar, dragged me to the curb and sat me down. He walked around the car, looking for bald tyres, I think. While this was going on, Dave Mason was still sat in the car shaking, while trying to stuff beer cans under the seat out of sight!

"The cop ran my ID and licence plate, but I was clean. He wrote me a ticket for making an unsafe turn and unsafe speed, and then told me to get the (expletive deleted!) out of here! I couldn't believe it – I thought Mason had had a heart attack by then!" And the licence plate on Gaskey's Ghia? It read "YERNEXT"…

Around 1982 or '83, the Karmann Ghia made way for a 1960 Beetle Cabriolet. The car, purchased from a guy in Irvine, had been the

finest examples of California Look style cars.

"We believed our stature (and egos!) in this microcosm of the hot-rod car culture of southern California was beyond reproach. If we were not the club with the best cars, the coolest and most fun individuals, or the most innovative and creative custom car builders, we believed and acted like we were. Looking back now at old photos of our Orange County group, I really have an overpowering sense of our arrogance and consistent authoritative mischief!

"Our weekly meetings at Perry's Pizza on Thursday nights were the comedic highlight of most of our weeks, and our bi-annual car rallies were absolutely legendary. The cars in our club were award-winning, trend-setting, insanely beautiful rides. We made a statement every-where we went. And that statement was made through a mixture of bravado and humour," Blaydes believes.

"For me, this can all be condensed into one experience at Bug-In 27. So here we were, another year, another Bug-In, another moment to make a statement to the VW world that we were a force to be reckoned with. Our cars had recently won some great awards, and our non-show cars, in turn, always placed well on the dragstrip. What was left for us to do? At an

earlier Thursday night club meeting it was decided that I, nicknamed "Worm", would enter the Mr Bug-In contest. Yes, the muscle-man contest that any person in his right mind would avoid at all costs. It should be made clear at this point that my physique was less than Adonis-like, as my nickname "Worm" might suggest. I was 6ft 2ins tall and a pipe-cleaner-like 134 pounds.

"A real party car" was how Glenn Gaskey described his Cabriolet!
(Glenn Gaskey)

Engine from the Ghia was installed but upgraded with an 82mm crank.
(Glenn Gaskey)

Great photo of Glenn Gaskey's 1960 Karmann Ghia ahead of Bill Schwimmer's "PEPTO" Squareback outside the Auto Haus store located at 1211 Tustin Avenue in Orange. (Glenn Gaskey)

"As I strode onto the drag strip, surrounded by a gaggle of huge men wearing tiny shorts, I was greeted by a chatty and ever-smiling Dyno Don Chamberlain (the original Mr Bug-in and now the event MC). Dyno was his typical self, deftly ridiculing me and the others as he introduced us to the crowd, who had to vote for the winner. I can recall standing next to this collosal human being, who was at least twice my breadth, all oiled up and glistening in the hot sun! Me? I just stood there in my baggy red plaid shorts, with my long skinny (and knobbly) legs poking out below, wearing a skin-tight yellow muscle tank top, which showed off my every rib.

"Dyno rallied the crowd in the OCIR stands to yell and clap for their favourite contestant, and he went down the line, one by one, pausing by each contender for the Mr Bug-In crown. When he eventually came to me, I recall the crowd began to chant: 'Worm! Worm! Worm!' My

Gaskey traded his Cabriolet for another Ghia, which featured the same 2180cc roller-crank motor with Drino Miller heads. The car was originally called Black Rushin' but when the floorpan was detailed and the chrome redone, it was renamed Brute Force. (Glenn Gaskey)

fellow club members were inciting this chant, which rapidly caught on. As you can imagine, I was quite the odd-one-out in this bunch of behemoths so, in the spirit of the occasion, I began to pose athletically – as any muscle contest contender should!

"I didn't, however, win the title that day, as it rightly went to another whose physique deserved it more. My consolation was a runner-up plaque and, of course, the pleasure derived from repre-senting DKK at the Bug-In! The fun part for us all was the very idea of sending a skinny kid to compete with the muscle-men in the hope of getting a laugh. It was another testament to our audacity and arrogance (and the sheer delight of being top dogs!), by acting as if the world was ours and we had a secret that no one else knew.

"Well, I guess in a way we did. Our 'secret' was the pride and sense of community each of us felt by being a part of this special group. Looking

After the second Ghia was stolen, Gasky eventually bought the red Notchback off Jim Moore. His brother Steve owned this pale blue Notchback, which was eventually wrecked on the 55 Freeway. (Glenn Gaskey)

The price you pay for leaving the colour choice to your brother... When Bill Schwimmer wanted his Squareback repainted following a vandal attack, it reappeared in a fetching shade of pink... (Bill Schwimmer)

95

Bill Schwimmer's first foray into the world of California Look was with this late-model Bug, to which he fitted repro EMPI eight-spoke wheels and a set of black T-bars. (Bill Schwimmer)

back, I would also have to say I believe that the real secret was our youth and ability to live for the moment, with the strength and determination to achieve something new. What a time, what an era, what a great group of friends!"

This sentiment is echoed by Mark Ramirez, a fellow DKK (or "Deek") member. "At the club meetings we would try to plan something to do every weekend – nothing formal, more a case of just whoever wanted to show up would be there, and it would always turn into a fun event. This was maybe something as simple as going to Hill-crest Park in Fullerton for a "wax on, wax off" cruise, or Craig Park in Brea for volleyball.

"I remember one occasion when we all headed to Eldorado Park. At the time, club member/founder Paul Harris was in the process of painting his Oval-window, but also wanted to attend the event. So he showed up with no door handles – and a beach chair for a seat! I crawled into his car from the passenger side and noticed there was no nut holding the steering-wheel on. With that, I pulled the wheel off and quietly shut the door, then had one of the members yell:

Freddie Desoto was a member of Der Kleiner Kampfwagens, alongside both Glenn Gaskey and Bill Schwimmer. Traditional dechromed bodywork contrasts with 1980s-style paint scheme. (Greg Brinton)

The T-bars were replaced by color-coded bumpers and Vittaloni mirrors – all very 1980s. Polished wheels were also popular at the time. (Bill Schwimmer)

'Hey Paul, you're car's rolling away', as I released the hand-brake so the car would roll forward downhill towards a creek.

"You should have seen him running to his car, screaming "Oh s**t!" You have to remember that he had no door handles or a steering- wheel to grab. When he saw my head pop up, I think he said some kind of nice words to me... Looking back, being part of Der Kleiner Kampfwagens was probably the most fun thing ever. The friendships we made in the club back then have lasted a lifetime."

Mark "Fred" Kessenich recollects his time in DKK: "I was in the club from 1979 to 1985. Like many VW clubs of the time, everyone had to get voted in on the strength of their car(s) and themselves. I met Dave McNew shortly after I bought my first car, which was a 1966 Beetle that I painted orange. Mark Ramirez was the President and Dave was vice-President. We used to meet at Larry's Pizza in Fullerton, but later we moved the meetings to a nearby Denny's restaurant. Looking back there were too many parties, Bug-Ins, Drag Days, cruise nights, car shows and car

Heavy graphic paint designs became commonplace in the '80s, completely going against the ultra-clean style that is recognised as the original California Look standard. (Greg Brinton)

Jim Moore's stunning Notchback was a real attention-getter in its day, and would still look good today. Car was sold to Glenn Gaskey and then equipped with a nitrous-injected turbo motor before being stolen and later recovered, stripped. (Greg Brinton)

rallies to recall them all, but I do remember it being a very fun time in my life."

"Fred" Kessenich converted his orange '66 sedan to European specification, including fitting a km/h speedometer, bumpers, deck-lid badge and Euro-spec Porsche 911 headlights. 'It also had early EMPI five-spokes that I sandblasted myself," Fred recalls. "The steering-wheel came from Gary Berg – it was an NOS (new old stock) EMPI GT, and I also had an NOS glass EMPI fuel filter. I built a blueprinted and balanced 1700cc engine for it while I was managing the Auto Haus store at Long Beach. It came with an Engle

110 cam, blueprinted stock oil pump, cc'd heads and 40mm Kadron carbs, with the jets reamed out as big as they'd go. It was my only transportation, but it ran hard for a small engine. I drove the Bug up and down the California coast, and to just about every VW event from 1979 to '85. It was a great car!"

On one occasion, the club took such a trip up north to a meeting: "On Friday August 29th, 1980, a few of us DKK members decided to drive up north to Sacramento for the Bug-O-Rama 5 event, which was due to be held two days later on the Sunday. Four of us opted to

Moore's Notchback was beautifully detailed and could hold its own at any show. It ran a 48IDA-equipped motor. Check the louvred rear apron and the clean tan-coloured interior. (Greg Brinton)

Costing a reputed $20,000 to build way back in 1983, Bobby Jackson's Peaches 'n' Scream *was a fully-detailed show car. (Greg Brinton)*

take our Cal Lookers on the road trip – Vince Ito, his brother Mark, Dave McNew and myself. Also along for the ride were club members Dave Fong, Brent Kooiman and Jeff Futomoko. We got there on Friday night, checked into our motel rooms and, of course, much partying took place to celebrate our successful arrival." There, Dave McNew's uncanny likeness to singer Tom Petty earned him a few beers – it just so happened that Petty was playing a concert in town that weekend! The next day, the group cleaned the bugs and road grime from their cars in the parking lot before heading into Old Sacramento to check out the scene.

"On Sunday we all headed off to the Bug-O-Rama at the Sacramento Raceway, where we displayed our cars in the car show – it was quite a trip, seeing how people reacted to us and our VWs. Remember, we came from southern California, and to us it felt like we had travelled back to 1970 in regards to how everyone dressed, looked – and how they presented their cars. Before we embarked on our journey, McNew thought it would be a fun idea to paint his valve covers white, after which he added different colour polka-dots for a 'Wonder Bread' effect. We all cracked up at the final result and felt it

Peaches 'n' Scream ran a set of VDO 'Jet Cockpit' *gauges in its filled dashboard. 2084cc engine pushed the car into the 'twelves'. (Stephan Szantai)*

One of the foremost VW accessory stores in its day, Johnny's Speed & Chrome on Beach Boulevard, Buena Park, prospered in the '80s but finally closed its doors in the early '90s. (Author)

Der Kleiner Kampfwagens members were each issued with these membership cards. (Stephan Szantai)

Caravanning to shows and race meetings was all part of life in DKK. (Mark Kessenich)

would turn some heads, for sure.

"Well, not only did people trip out on our Devo and Ramones (two of our favourite bands at the time) shirts and pins, but now they really had something to stick in their minds. I remember cracking up as we watched them walking around our cars, then they'd make their way to Dave's Bug and peek underneath the engine to do a double-take at his valve covers. It

was classic!"

As with the Bug-Ins, club members were keen to participate in as many events as they could, recalls Kessenich. "They had this Bug Push event, where teams had to push a VW Beetle down the drag strip. Seeing that it was in the middle of a typical California summer, it was extremely hot. One of our guys, Jeff, decided to run out there barefoot and help push one of the cars. Needless to say, his feet were grilled on the hot asphalt and were very blistered. He had to ride back to our motel in Mark's Bus, with both feet resting on the dash."

Many club members over the years have had run-ins with the police – it seems to have been par for the course for Cal Look owners back in the 1970s and '80s. Not all cops were intent on causing hassle, though, as Mark Kessenich found out. "That night, we went back to Old Sacto, but I couldn't get in the bar because I was too young, so I thought I would find my own way back to the motel. Wrong! I ended up going way north and drove for what seemed like for ever. After an hour or so, I felt it was best to turn around, as it was almost midnight and there was no one else on the freeway to ask for directions. I was doing about 100mph down a country road when I saw a cop's lights in my mirrors. I pulled over and was actually glad to find someone to ask for directions. I thought for sure he was

Mark "Fred" Kessenich's 1965 sedan was converted to "European" look, with decklid badge, shorty over-riders and orange-topped turn signals. Car ran on a set of EMPI five-spokes and packed a 1700cc engine. (Mark Kessenich)

Exhibitions of speed, or a settling of scores, was a popular Friday or Saturday night pastime… (Suzy Herbert)

going to write me a speeding ticket. Instead, he was totally cool and asked how come my car was going so fast!

"After I showed him the engine, he told me he was impressed by how clean everything on the car was. He told me the way back to the motel and then suggested that I get a new month sticker for my licence plate, because it was faded. He'd given me a break after I explained to him that I'd travelled up to Sacramento for a car show. I counted my blessings that night and drove back slowly.

"For most of us, it was our first long car trip away from home. Remember, we were all only 18 or so at the time. We came back home with great memories, plenty of photos, and McNew acquired a new nickname. Some of us still call him 'TP' or 'Petty'."

Of course, being part of DKK meant more than just partying at an event. There was the matter of "honour" to take care of – the honour of the Volkswagen, that is. "One night', says Kessenich, 'we were all cruising Whittier Blvd. McNew and I had parked our Beetles and Kevan Wood let us drive his extremely clean Karmann Ghia convertible. It had a small (1600, or maybe 1641cc) engine, but with reworked heads, 48IDAs, a Berg transmission and a merged Four-Tuned header. With Dave driving, a guy pulled up next to us at a light in a black Camaro or Fire-

Dave McNew – also known as TP or Petty to his friends in deference to his likeness to singer Tom Petty – decided to paint his valve covers in the style of Wonderloaf packaging. Well, it was certainly different! (Mark Kessenich)

The cars of – from left to right – Greg Brinton, Bill Schwimmer and Dave Mason formed the nucleus of the third generation of Der Kleiner Panzers. Each was a potent, street-legal California Looker. (Greg Brinton)

bird, and started making fun of the Ghia saying: 'Ha, ha! Look at the kraut-can!' as he rapped off his engine.

"As the light turned green, Dave stomped on the gas pedal and we left that dude way behind. I couldn't stop laughing my ass off. At the next light, the guy was pissed off and asked us what we were running for an engine. We calmly told him it was a 1600. He didn't believe us and swore that we had nitrous oxide. We assured him that we didn't and it was just a really well balanced and blueprinted engine. I'll never forget that night or the look on that guy's face – being beaten by a Ghia with the top down!"

Todd Fuller owned three Cal Lookers, two of which were while he was a member of DKK. "I got bitten by the VW Bug after I'd put together a Cal Look VW for my girlfriend. I then built myself a 1967 Bug, a '67 Ghia and a '65 sunroof sedan, all of which were 'Lookers'. The last two were even featured in some magazines at the time and won a few shows.

"I lived in the San Gabriel Valley and tried to hook up with a few local clubs, but their views weren't quite the same. This was around 1978 or 1979, and although I may have seen a 'Panzer' car here and there, I had never really seen a full assembly of DKP club members' rides. One night

I was at a local cruise spot, out between San Gabriel Valley and Orange County, when I met Dave McNew of DKK.

"He seemed really cool and took me over to Orange County (Cal Look centre of the universe!) to check out a meeting – I was hooked! The cars were the cleanest, people were the coolest, girls were the hottest… Hey, we were in Orange County, after all!"

There was definitely a sense of pride being in the club: "Just having DKK decals on your car got you the full respect of all your peers. After I joined, at least six of my friends put together cars and joined, too. We had the craziest Halloween parties, the best rallies and show 'n' shines (they were lots of work, but really worth it). And even when we weren't putting on an event, we were meeting every weekend so we could play volleyball, socialize or help each other with our projects."

However, the number one aim was always to have the best club representation at the Bug-Ins. When these legendary events at Orange Country International Raceway eventually came to an end in 1983, it was as if the heart had been ripped out of the club scene in the 1980s. People made every effort to get to the show, even if it meant that they had to work non-stop

for a week to make it. Another "Deek", Rick Meredith, knew this scenario only too well: "I worked for the BAP Geon Imported Car Parts store in Anaheim, and the corporate management scheduled a companywide inventory the Friday before the Fall Bug-In – every year! So not only did I have to worry about getting my car done, but I also had to balance that with my employer's demand on my time."

But Rick wasn't gong to let the small matter of work get in the way of play, especially where club involvement was concerned. "One year I got way behind schedule for getting my '67 Beetle ready for the event, but Bug-In was our Holy Grail and I was determined to do everything in my power to get there. So, on the Friday before, I drove my Notchback into the auto parts store at 7.30am. After a draining day of counting thousands of screws, Weber jets, brake springs and trying to identify unmarked parts, I headed home at midnight.

"I stepped into the garage and surveyed the job ahead of me. My '67 was up on jack-stands, the wheels were off, the deck-lid was off and the brakes were apart. The 1776 engine was sitting next to the car, completely – and I mean completely – disassembled, to the point where the rods weren't even on the crank and the

pistons not on the rods. So I began assembling the motor and, by 3.00am Saturday morning, I had the case buttoned up. I decided that I was at a good point to stop and grab a little sleep.

"My alarm went off at 7.00am and the next 36 hours were a blur. Running on four hours sleep in a 60-hour span does that! I can't recall how many DKK members showed up on that Saturday/Sunday morning, but the garage was in constant motion, with four, five or six people working on the car at a time. Not only did they help with my car, but they took time away from working on their own cars – and they made sure that everyone had food and drinks, and that I had all the parts I needed.

"I especially remember Bill Schwimmer, Henry Mayeda and Robbie Blake putting in long hours that day, but there was lots of others. At about 3.00am Sunday morning I started sending everyone off to Orange County International Raceway, which was about six miles from my house. I certainly didn't want them to miss out on Bug-In, plus we had to arrive as a group so we could park together. They promised to save me a spot and went on their way. I toiled away for the next four hours and soon the night started to fade into daylight. I had become a robot, crossing items off checklists.

Greg Brinton's '67 was originally built by Gary Grauman and purchased by Brinton in 1988. Within a few years, he installed a 217bhp 2175cc motor with SuperFlo heads and a Berg five-speed transmission. (Greg Brinton)

Cabriolets have never played a major role in the California Look scene, primarily because they have only rarely been used for drag racing. Few could deny, though, just how good they can look…
(Greg Brinton)

"At about a quarter-to-seven, I had run out of things to cross off my list. I gave the car the once-over and made sure that we hadn't missed anything, then took out my static timing light and set the 010 distributor. I pushed the car out onto the driveway, took the covers off the 48s, pulled the power to the coil and cranked the car until I got oil pressure. It looked good, so I decided to give it a try.

"On the second crank, the sound of my unmuffled 1776 echoed off the hills around my house. Sure, the neighbours were going to be pissed, but I didn't care! I had done it! After a quick break-in period, I took a quick shower, donned a fresh DKK club shirt and was on my way. Down Browning to Irvine Boulevard – easy on the throttle because it's all residential – then left on Irvine. Within a half mile I was out in the farmers' fields, so I could finally open it up. It sounded great!

"I continued out to Sand Canyon, where I made a right and headed down to the track entrance. Since I was there late, the line was manageable and, by 9.00am, I was in the car show area. I pulled up to the DKK club display

and took the spot that had been saved for me. I pulled my lawn chair out of the trunk, opened the car up for the show and then collapsed into the chair. My 24-hour sleepless thrash had been worth it, but more important was that the club had come together to make sure that no one missed out. We may have drooled over the cars, but it's people that were – and still are – truly special. And it only took me a 14-hour sleep session to recover!"

Just when everyone thought the party would go on for ever, news broke that Orange County International Raceway was going to close. That in itself was a sad sign of the times, as land became more valuable for industrial and housing development but, for the die-hard VW enthusiast, the news was nothing short of a tragedy. No OCIR meant no Bug-In. No Bug-In meant no focal point in the club's year. The last Bug-In was scheduled for April 1983, and members wanted to make sure they were ready.

"We had the reputation as the club to beat when it came to Bug-In, especially when it came to being the Most Represented. We had won that award for Bug-Ins 28, 29 and 30, consecutively.

We knew that 31 was going to be the last one, and we wanted to make sure that we put a huge DKK stamp on this final event. Since this was my second term as Club President, it was especially important to me that we were most represented. The past Most Rep awards had been won with around 25 cars, but I wanted a number that left no doubt – one that could never be matched. The number that came to mind was 45…

"We sat down at a club meeting and outlined our strategy. Keep in mind that we had about 18 active members at the time, so we were talking about substantially more than double our active membership. Our ally was the phone – we started calling old members and friends six weeks before the event. We were beating the bushes for every possible car. Every member did what he could.

"The night before the Bug-In we met at Denny's on State College to drive down as a group. There were a lot of cars – an initial count put the total at 42, including cars we knew would be meeting us there. Our caravan of almost 40 VWs hit the freeway, and soon we were at the entrance to OCIR. We took our place in line and got ready for the night ahead of us.

"We tapped the first beer keg and started the party – and it was a party that lasted until the wee small hours, before it was time to try to grab some sleep. My Savannah Beige '67 was parked next to Bill Schwimmer's Pepto Squareback and, as Bill was shorter than me, he could lay out in the back of the Squareback, while I'd been forced to wad up a pillow next to the B-pillar in my '67 and sleep sitting in the driver's seat.

"I was woken by the sound of hundreds of Volkswagens starting, so we all moved along to the pit entrance and started the 'VW push' – because the queue was long, we pushed our cars rather than starting them, moving two car lengths at a time, until the people ahead had filled out their paperwork and paid for their entrance ticket.

"At the end of the day, we gathered around to hear the final awards with great anticipation. They announced that we'd won Most Represented Club – with a final count 47 cars!"

So, the 1980s wasn't the cultural wasteland that some people would have us believe – here we have clear evidence that there were still some very fast cars cruising the streets of Orange County, and devoted club members who wanted nothing more than to keep the true California Look spirit alive.

Rick Meredith looks back on those times with a sense of nostalgia. "DKK was all about good friends, cool cars and having the best possible time – even if it meant getting into some mischief (and, boy, did we!). It was a great time and the bonds we formed still tie us together today. Recently, I've hooked up with several members that I'd lost track of over the years… and we picked up our friendships after 20 years apart as if no time has passed at all."

Ken Cervone's IDA-equipped Cabriolet is as much a Cal Looker as any other VW featured in this chapter. And let's face it, what car could be better than a Cabriolet for cruising the streets of Orange County? (Greg Brinton)

Chapter 9

SCHWIMMING AGAINST THE TIDE

"I thought I was going to go through the back window of that thing – I'd never launched so hard in my life..."
Bill Schwimmer

1980s

I n the mid 1980s, Bill Schwimmer drove what to everyone's way of thinking was a pretty neat Volkswagen Squareback (Type 3 Variant). It was, in his words, "A decent car which received loads of attention, both magazine-wise and while driving out on the street – but it wasn't quite what I was after."

Having grown up in Southern California, Bill had a long-held interest in the hot-rod scene, with a particular leaning towards traditional cars such as fenderless '32 Ford hi-boys and the like. To him, the stripped-down no-nonsense style was the height of cool, so it probably comes as

little surprise that, as neat as his Squareback might have been, he had his sights set on building a traditional California Look VW. "I really wanted to build a true California Look car in terms of both appearance and performance," recounts Schwimmer, "and I really wanted something to put a set of BRM wheels on. The Squareback just wasn't it!"

It's worth mentioning at this point that the Squareback began life in Bill's hands as a pretty typical 1980s-style 'Looker', with bright-red paintwork and a set of polished EMPI eight-spoke wheels. It was a great looking car, which

Squarebacks were never a popular choice but, like the owner of this stunning red example on original EMPI Spyder Mags, Bill Schwimmer saw the potential offered by the VW Variant. Check the colour-coded bumpers and polished wheels – typical 1980s touches. (Bill Schwimmer)

certainly attracted a lot of interest – unfortunately, some of that interest was from the wrong kind of person, and the paintwork was vandalised one night. As his brother, Randy, was a painter by trade, Schwimmer was happy to hand the car over for a complete repaint. "The trouble is, like many sprayers, Randy said he'd choose the colour… I didn't mind, but had no idea what to expect."

The end result was a pink car that became instantly known as "Pepto", after the similarly-coloured Peptobismol anti-acid medicine. It

Schwimmer's first foray into VWs was this late-model Beetle, with blacked-out trim and repro eight-spokes. (Bill Schwimmer)

Following the vandalism incident, Schwimmer handed the car to his brother for a repaint, leaving the colour choice up to the painter. The end result was startling, to say the least! with "Pepto" pink paint and polished alloys. (Bill Schwimmer)

Although he liked the Squareback, Schwimmer really wanted a car with which he could create his own Looker. He swapped the Type 3 for this 1955 Oval-window, which initially ran a nitrous-injected 1776 motor and EMPI "fives". (Bill Schwimmer)

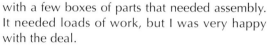

The Oval soon became a high-maintenance street racer, with a variety of engines, beginning with a 2017cc unit with 11.0:1 Fumio Fukaya heads, dual 48IDAs and an Engle FK89 cam. (Bill Schwimmer)

looked great, in a 1980s kind of fashion, and even made it onto the cover of the August 1984 edition of *VW Greats* magazine. But, deep down, Bill knew it wasn't what he really wanted. "I traded the Squareback for a 1955 Oval-window in January 1986 to a guy named Wade. He got a totally finished magazine cover car and I got something that ran and drove, had a set of polished EMPI five-spoke replicas and came

with a few boxes of parts that needed assembly. It needed loads of work, but I was very happy with the deal.

"When I first bought it, the car was already running a 1776cc motor with dual 48IDA Weber carburettors, a fully-plumbed-in nitrous oxide system and a gearbox with a low 4.86:1 final drive. I had a little bodywork done, along with some paintwork, and it turned into a very presentable car. I took it down the strip at Bakersfield with the 1776 on 165 radial tyres and it went 14.80s. I never did try the nitrous system, even though it was fully plumbed, as I always thought it was sort of cheating."

Most people would be pretty happy with a street car which ran fourteens but Bill Schwimmer wanted something even quicker. "I was room-mates with Dave Voegtly at the time, and we lived behind his parents' house where his brother Mark lived. As Mark worked for Gene Berg, he assembled the parts for a 2-litre motor that I had acquired. It was a 78.4mm x 90.5mm (2017cc) deal with a pair of 42mm x 37.5mm heads that had been reworked by Fumio Fukaya Enterprises out at Riverside. It ran the dual 48IDAs, an Engle FK89 camshaft and an 11.0:1 compression ratio. The only problem was that the crank and flywheel weren't wedge-mated, relying instead on just eight 8mm

dowels.

"Mark said it wouldn't hold – and he was right. I remember the first time we took it to the track – it was actually my first time down the strip with some power and slicks. Mark told me to 'Get yourself set in the car', but I was thinking this is no big deal… I did a burnout and staged the car, brought the motor up and let it fly. Well, I thought I was going to go through the back window of that thing – I'd never launched so hard in my life. In fact, it blew my foot clear off the throttle. I gained much more respect for what was going on that day. Two passes later the flywheel came off the crankshaft. I learned to listen after that…"

Voegtly and Schwimmer set about rebuilding the motor, making sure this time to have the crank and flywheel assembly wedgemated. They used a new crankcase and cut the cylinder heads for higher compression, losing a cooling fin in the process. As the proud owner recalls: "It had about 13.0:1 now – we got it running and it was just stupidly fast. I first ran that version in early 1987 at Las Vegas and it ran 12.50s right away, with me still learning how to drive it. It revved so fast it was hard to keep up with. In fact, it would sometimes flash to 10,000rpm in the burnout – and as much as 9500rpm in first gear, but it was a total rush to drive. It really took

my breath away off the line…"

Schwimmer raced the Oval with the polished five-spokes for a while, but in May 1987 he realized his dream by purchasing his first set of magnesium BRM wheels. "This set actually came off Mark Hunsaker's 1966 Bug that was featured in the June 1976 issue of *Hot VWs* magazine. I could have purchased the whole car for $1900 but all I wanted was the wheels. In the

Original BRM wheels were purchased for $900 back in 1987. (Bill Schwimmer)

Hunt magneto, IDAs, Berg linkage and Berg pulley were all used. (Bil Schwimmer)

To the unsuspecting owner of a domestic V8, there were few clues as to the performance potential of the tan-coloured Oval. Full bumpers and side trim belied the true nature of the beast…
(Bill Schwimmer)

Bill Schwimmer describes how he tried to make the engine look a little "cheesy" by fitting some cheap chrome parts and sticking surf decals to the tinware – that way, it would arouse less interest among the V8 crowd, who would then fall easy pray to the VW. (Bill Schwimmer)

end, I paid $900 for them, which was quite a bit of money at the time – in fact, that was all my money at the time! But it made my vision complete."

Bill raced the Oval-window at some West Coast VW events and V8 nostalgia drag races. He also street raced it around some of the more popular meeting places in Orange County, including Sand Canyon, where the roads are wide, straight and deserted at night, or around the infamous Nabsico factory. Most races were for bragging rights, but others were for money –

perhaps just one or two hundred bucks, but enough to show serious intent. "Street racing isn't something I would want glorified, but it happened a lot back then," recalls Schwimmer. In some of the photographs of the car, it's possible to see the engine and how, by today's' standards, it appears rather innocuous. "I used to stick old surf decals on the chrome fan-shroud just to make it look kinda cheesy. That way, unless you really knew what you were looking at, the engine didn't appear to be anything special. It helped fool a lot of the V8 guys into

135x15 Pirelli Cinturatos were fitted to the polished and detailed BRMs at the front…

LeCarra steering wheels and AutoMeter Monster tachs with a shift light were becoming popular by the late 1980s. Aside from these additions, the dashboard of the Oval was stock. (Bill Schwimmer)

thinking I was easy pickings!"

By this time, the Oval-window was to all intents and purposes a race car on the street, but it did get driven locally – or trailered to more distant venues before being unloaded to make an appearance at an event. "It was a blast to drive, but I really wanted something a bit more streetable. Suddenly, version two was on the horizon." The final specification of the car in its first incarnation included an Ed's Machine 78.4mm crankshaft, Cima 90.5mm cylinders and pistons, Racer's Choice welded 42x37.5 heads (reworked by Fumio Fukaya), VW rods, Engle FK89 cam, 48IDAs, Vertex magneto, 1.625in S&S header and an A1 2.5in turbo muffler. In this form, the car ran a best elapsed time of 12.00secs at sea-level, and 12.23secs at Palmdale, which was at some 3500 feet. According to the NHRA's altitude correction factor, this was equivalent to an 11.83 at sea-level. The best terminal speed the 1750lb car reached was 110mph at Fremont Raceway, near San Francisco.

Although obviously happy with the perform-

Who wouldn't look happy driving such a car? The problem for Bill Schwimmer was that the Oval evolved into a race car on the street and he began tiring of running a high-compression "race gas motor". The engine was detuned for street use. (Bill Schwimmer)

…while 205/65 Cinturatos were used on the rear. Doubtless, they struggled for grip (Bill Schwimmer)

Make no bones about it, Bill Schwimmer's Oval was a fearsome machine, easily capable of pulling the front wheels on every launch.
(Bill Schwimmer)

On slicks, the Oval ran low-twelves at altitude, reckoned to be equal to 11-second passes at sea level. Impressive, yes?
(Bill Schwimmer)

ance, Schwimmer was growing tired of running a car that demanded the use of race fuel at $3 a gallon. "I wanted something I could drive around. Mark Voegtly had a set of 44mm x 37.5mm heads that had been done by Dean and Marla Lowry, and set up for pump gas. I traded him for the race heads and we replaced the original camshaft with an Engle FK87. We also dropped the compression ratio to a more modest 8.5:1. Even in this state of tune, the motor still made 173bhp on Roger Crawford's dyno at only 6000rpm, but it would still pull to about 8000rpm – we just never took it up that high on the dyno.

"I put radials on the Berms (BRMs) and fitted a nice interior from Whittier's Auto Interiors,

which was next to Roger's shop – this is now West Coast Classics. I drove it around like this for a while and it was a blast. It would totally annihilate the radials at will! I street raced it here and there like this, as well. The only time I drag raced this combo was at Carlsbad, where it went 13.52 at 105mph – it was a bit 'traction limited', to say the least! On slicks I am sure it would have run easy mid-12s without issue."

Bill drove the revised Oval around as a street car for a few months, but felt that it didn't quite fit in at the VW events – it was much too plain for most people's tastes at the time. He would regularly take it to V8 cruise nights, where it was far better received. He recalls that: "The V8 guys that had seen it run were also terrified of it! I think that is why they respected it." Greg Brinton, Dave Mason and Schwimmer would go to car shows together with DKP decals in the rear quarter-windows of their Beetles, "Because we wanted to emulate the cars we saw when we were kids." The trio went on to form the third generation of the famous Orange County-based VW club, once they had received the blessing of former members, including Ron Fleming.

"I went through cars pretty often back then and, as I didn't drive the Oval-window for a little while, I didn't think I would miss it. After talking with Dyno Don, I sold the car in February 1989 to someone in Japan for just $7500, turnkey. After that, I bought a Porsche 356 replica from event promoter Dick Adams and drove that for a while. But I soon realized that wasn't what I was about. I saw an advert in the local *Recycler*

paper for a 'Grey rag-top with red interior', which sounded pretty cool. It turned out that the ad was wrong – the car (which, coincidentally, was being offered by Dyno Don) was actually Coral Red with a grey interior. I wasn't too sure about it at first, but decided to go ahead after I thought about it for a while."

The Coral Red Beetle has gone on to become one of the best-known cars in the California Look scene today, with its detailed BRM wheels, "stroker" motor and Berg five-speed transmission. It may not be quite the drag strip terror that Bill's tan-coloured Oval once was, but it's a driver – and a keeper. It's also a far cry from a Pepto-pink Squareback…

Dialed in at 12.30secs, the Oval launches hard off the line at Seattle International Raceway on one of Schwimmer's many trips north. (Bill Schwimmer)

The Godfather of modern VW performance, the late Dean Lowry, poses with Schwimmer's current ride – Coral Red rag-top. (Author)

Chapter 10

ANATOMY OF A RACE CAR

"It is important to realise that most race cars were built for one purpose, and one purpose alone: to go fast."

Chromed Porsche rims and a push-bar on the rear are about the only obvious modifications made to Darrell Vittone's street car as it evolved into a drag racer – engine modifications were modest at this stage, too. (Glenn Miller)

It is an irrefutable fact that the California Look style developed as a direct consequence of what was happening on the drag strips of southern California. Prior to the arrival on the scene of cars like the original *Inch Pincher* and *Deano Dyno-Soar* Gassers, there were few street-driven cars with lowered front suspension, dechromed bodywork or, one could argue, high-compression motors hooked up to close-ratio transmissions.

Although we have come across at least one magazine reference to a VW competing as early as 1954, Volkswagens didn't become a regular sight on America's drag strips until the early 1960s. It's not hard to figure out why this should be so: there was a lack of quality speed equipment at the time. Engine conversions from companies such as Okrasa – an acronym of *Öettinger Kraftfahrttechnische Spezialanstalt* – in Germany (available via EMPI in the USA) were largely geared towards street or rally use, and lacked the explosive power deemed necessary for drag race success. Only when enthusiasts such as Dean Lowry began to modify components specifically for strip use did we begin to see a turning of the tide.

Dean Lowry and Darrell Vittone shelter from the sun in the EMPI pick-up while waiting in line to make another pass in the car which went on to become the world famous Inch Pincher. (Glenn Miller)

For people like Lowry, the starting point would be the tried-and-tested (on the Autobahn, at least) 30bhp (36hp SAE) engine used from 1954 onwards. In engineering terms, this was in a jewel of a motor, but sadly lacking in both outright power and ultimate strength. The crankshafts were weak and showed a propensity for breaking when run at sustained high rpm – high, in this instance, being anything much over 5500rpm… The con-rods were prone to failure, too. Porsche had overcome some of the weaknesses by developing roller-bearing crankshafts, which allowed the engine to turn at much higher rpm, but they could not handle high compression. Roller bearings may have been excellent at withstanding momentary oil starvation under hard cornering, but that was about all. And the con-rods were little better than stock VW forg-

Although the majority of sedan-based race cars were capable of self-starting, NHRA regulations required them to be equipped with a push bar if bumpers were not fitted so they could be push started in an emergency. (Glenn Miller)

ings, too.

As far as plain-bearings cranks were concerned, there was none better than the forged "stroker" produced by Okrasa. Used with stock cylinders, this resulted in a swept volume of 1285cc – better than 1192cc, but not by much! A more expensive alternative was to use the crankshaft from a pre-1954 Porsche 356, which offered a stroke of 74mm.

Lowry tried to overcome the problem of con-rods splitting, thanks to stresses induced by compression or detonation, by building up the I-beam section with weld, or by boxing them with sheet metal. Both methods dramatically increased the weight of the rod, placing an even greater strain on the bottom end, and were not the answer. When SPG made an aftermarket roller-bearing crank available, it appeared to offer a solution to some of the problems suffered by early drag racers, but not all. In fact, SPG cranks suffered their own problems – the crank was built up in sections, each being pressed together. This was fine for a road or circuit race application, but proved weak in drag race situations where the shock load generated by dropping the clutch on the start line could be sufficient to cause the crank to twist.

However, the greatest legacy left to the world

Most drag cars of the 1960s and early '70s began life as street cars, and the famous Underdog was no exception. It started out as Doug Gordon's daily driver but ended up as one of the best-known race cars of all time, driven by Ron Fleming. (Ron Fleming)

of VW performance was the so-called "SPG-pattern" flywheel dowel set-up. Whereas the stock VW crank was drilled to accept just four indexing dowels to locate the flywheel, SPG cranks – and almost all subsequent aftermarket products – came pre-drilled to accept eight dowels. One of the dowels was slightly offset, meaning that the flywheel could only be fitted in one position, therefore ensuring the assembly remained in balance following an engine rebuild.

"Eight-dowelling" stock cranks, or the more desirable Okrasa forgings, became accepted as a simple but effective solution to the problem of the flywheel tearing itself loose from the end of the crankshaft. Porsche had recognised this as a problem many years earlier, largely as a consequence of the "on-off" use of the throttle in road-race and rally applications, but Volkswagen never changed its design. After all, the Beetle was never intended to be a sports car, let alone a drag-race competitor.

Inch Pincher Too *was one of the best-prepared of all VW drag racers. Its Molly-applied paintwork made it a real standout. (Jere Alhadeff/Hot VWs)*

In the background lies the abandoned bodyshell of the first Inch Pincher, *while* Inch Pincher Too *and the EMPI VSR await their fate after the sale of EMPI to Filter Dynamics. BRM wheels abound…* **(Author's collection)**

From south of the border came Pancho Mendoza and Pink Panther, a car which is alive and kicking today in Germany. Spindle-mount wheels were a popular way to save weight, albeit at the expense of braking efficiency. Short wheelie-bars were common at the time. (Jere Alhadeff/Hot VWs)

The introduction of the all-new 34bhp (40-horse) engine in 1960 overcame many of the inherent weaknesses of the original 30bhp motor, but it was still not ideal. However, the new 1500cc engine, first seen in the new Type 3 range in 1961, marked a turning point in the performance industry, as the old adage "there's no substitute for cubic inches" never held more true. The longer (69mm) stroke crankshaft and improved "311" con-rods (the part number a reference to their origins in the Type 3 range) were far stronger than anything previously available from the factory. Improved cylinder heads also made a huge difference in the potential

Wisps of smoke from the tyres as Dean Lowry powers off the line in the Deano Dyno-Soar Gasser. 13-inch front wheels were used on many cars in the late '60s as a way to reduce weight and lower the front end to improve aeodynamic stability (Jere Alhadeff/Hot VWs)

power output of any race or road-driven VW.

Boosting the capacity further was possible using a long-stroke crankshaft (SPG, Okrasa, or a independently-produced "welded" stroker), or by enlarging the cylinders – or both. Porsche cylinders could be used, but were expensive and unpopular for that reason. Porsche 80mm cylinders (from the 1500 model) resulted in a capacity of approximately 1300cc when used with a stock VW crank, while the larger 82.5mm cylinders (Porsche 1600) created a 1500cc VW engine. The cheap option was to fit the cylinders and modified pistons from a Chevrolet Corvair engine. Early (1960) versions came with 86mm cylinders, while the later type had 88mm bores. The latter could be bored out to 90mm, using specially-cast pistons from J&E in Los Angeles, a company well-known today in VW circles. This led to EMPI (in association with the German company, Mahle) to market its own "big-bore" kits for both 30bhp and 34bhp engines – and later, the 1500 unit.

Incidentally, as an aside, although the Okrasa crankshaft has always been regarded as a masterpiece of German engineering, the first such crank was, in fact, designed for Öettinger by one Cliff Collins, an American who was a partner in the then well-known Harman-Collins speedshop, which specialised in tuning domestic vehicles.

From little acorns... This sorry-looking bodyshell was used to create the second version of the Underdog *(Jim Edmiston)*

119

New-look Underdog *with its psychadelic paintwork leaves the line at OCIR.*
(Jim Holmes)

A few years later, the same car lies abandoned behind FAT's workshops. It was eventually stripped of its identity and sold off…
(Jim Holmes)

So what might be the specification of a typical drag racer of the early- to mid-1960s? By today's standards, the one word that comes to mind is "unsophisticated". Typically, one might find a 1500cc engine equipped with a forged plain-bearing Okrasa or SPG roller-bearing crankshaft. In the case of the former, polished 311-style con-rods would be the norm. The crankcase would remain pretty much stock with, at best, a by-pass oil-filter system. The cylinder heads – remember, this is before the VW "dual-port" head was introduced – would benefit from a full port and polish and, more likely than not, be Okrasa or the more exotic Denzel in origin, as these were both dual-port castings. The compression ratio would be set as high as 12.0:1, placing incredible strain on the stock con-rods, but it was a small price to pay for the power benefits gained.

Camshafts would typically be reground from factory castings, and there were several options available to the would-be racer. Weber Cams offered the 105-V for competition use. This was a dual-lobe cam, with 257 degrees of duration on the inlet, and 245 degrees on the exhaust. The lift was advertised as being 0.325in and the cam was reckoned to be good for up to 7000rpm, although presumably not in an engine with a stock crankshaft! Racer Brown's 15-A camshaft came with 254 degrees of duration and 0.307in lift, while the Iskendarian VW 228 promised 264 degrees duration and 0.315in lift. Howard Cams' VW-9A sported a similar 264 degrees duration and 0.314in lift.

Carburation was relatively restricted in choice in the early 1960s, with dual Zenith 32NDIX carburettors from a Porsche being popular – and about the ultimate choice for an all-out race engine, too. This is one reason why racers like Dean Lowry experimented with using Shorrocks superchargers, for they compensated for the lack of airflow offered by the relatively small Zenith carbs. Only when the 48IDA Weber carburettor became readily available in the later 1960s did the VW Performance industry begin to turn its back on the blower as a simple way to extract

Some 25 years or more after its demise, the tower at Orange County International Raceway still remains an iconic image in VW history. Steve Tims' Mean Machine *Ghia gets the drop on a Buggy...* (Roger Grago)

the most from the least. In fact, even as late as 1968, the hot set-up on the drag strip was still the Shorrocks-blown VW motor (with those Corvair-derived cylinders) or a tuned Porsche engine, as borne out by contemporary magazine features on two front-running racers (EMPI's *Inch Pincher* and Ray Groom's *Glass Wag'n*).

The weakest link was – and would be for many years – the VW transmission. The big problem was that there were no commercially-available close-ratio gear sets for the Beetle's transaxle, prompting many racers to turn to Porsche's similar 356 unit. This had the added advantage of allowing a wide range of factory-offered ratios to be used. ZF limited-slip differential units were a bonus, too. Axles? You polished them – and broke them...

By the end of the decade, though, things had changed dramatically, with dual 48IDA Webers becoming the induction system of choice. Taking Dean Lowry's 1968-built *Deano Dyno-Soar* race car as an example, we can see how engines had become far more sophisticated in the matter of just a few short years. Starting with a factory 1500 unit, Lowry built a 2180cc based around an SPG roller-bearing crankshaft and a set of his own 92mm cast-iron cylinders. The camshaft was a DDS grind, sporting a far more radical 300 degrees of duration and 0.360in lift. Lightened cam followers were also used. The cylinder heads were reworked VW dual-ports,

with 40mm inlet valves – about the biggest that were available at the time – and match-ported to a pair of short Deano manifolds carrying dual 48IDA Weber carburettors. The exhaust system was a DDS special, while ignition was taken care of by a Vertex magneto – the popular choice among racers for the next 25 or more years. Other details included a DDS-developed full-flow oiling system based around a modified VW oil pump, and a windage tray to limit oil surge in the sump.

The transmission used by Lowry was pirated from a 1964 Porsche 356, with ratios chosen to match the 27in-diameter slicks, which were

Ken Jevec, at the wheel of his Oval window sedan, samples a little Wednesday night grudge race action at OCIR.
(Ken Jevec)

Probably one of the nicest-looking and best-detailed drag racers was Lee Leighton's sedan. Simple, single-colour paintwork and BRM wheels clearly demonstrate the cross-over between race car and California Look (Roger Grago)

Greg Aronson driving the as yet unfinished rag-top sedan which became the seminal California Looker at OCIR. The rear wheels are blue-painted BRMs from the **Underdog.** *(Jim Holmes)*

mounted on DDS spun-aluminium rims, those at the front measuring just 13in in diameter.

The secret to the success of cars such as the Dyno-Soar was their low weight. With a relatively small capacity engine, the car needed to be light to be competitive within the NHRA (National Hot Rod Association) "Gas" classes, where individual sub-classes were determined on a weight per cubic inch basis. Lowry began by gutting the car of its factory interior, then removing much of the internal metalwork, including the dashboard. Cars of this era were not pretty and the term 'hack job' could have been coined especially to describe the early Volkswagen Gassers.

There was a class requirement for each car to run headlights – but the rules didn't say they had to be the original lights, or even that they had to work. Lowry replaced the original headlamps with dummies, and installed motorcycle units in the front fenders to meet the regulations.

Every effort was made to remove weight, almost – or so it seems in retrospect – regardless of the consequences regarding safety… Brake backing plates were drilled to within an inch of their life, steel floorpans were cut from the chassis to be replaced by unsupported sheets of aluminium, and front wheels were mounted on cut-down empty brake drums. As history was to prove, probably the most dubious change made was to hack off the original front axle beam and replace it with a lightweight "funny car-style" tubular axle. Ultimately, this front-end set-up would be blamed for causing a near-fatal roll-over accident which destroyed the original Dyno-Soar. With Plexiglas replacing the original windows, the 11-second car tipped the scales at a race-ready 1150lbs – almost 500lbs lighter than stock. Like so many cars of its time, with over 200bhp on tap and only a basic understanding of vehicle aerodynamics available, it was an accident waiting to happen.

By the early 1970s, a formula for a successful Volkswagen had been pretty much adopted across the board. The Fleming and Gordon *Underdog* I/Gas sedan was a good example of an early 1970s Gasser, with its unchopped roof, BRM wheels and almost factory appearance. But

Bear Barrilleaux lifts the wheels off the line at Pomona during the NHRA Winternationals. Wonder if the driver of the Corvette was ready to be beaten by a Bug? Bracket racing provided a level playing field which allowed humble VWs to embarrass far bigger machinery. (Jere Alhadeff/Hot VWs)

that appearance was deceptive, for under the skin lay a highly-modified drag racer in a similar vein to the DDS car before it. Technology had moved on, though, with a plain-bearing Revmaster crankshaft used in place of the old SPG roller crank so beloved of the first VW racers. Porsche con-rods became widely used, with their slim profile, smaller journal diameter and lighter weight making them a better choice for use with a stroker crank inside a stock VW

One of the sharpest-looking cars ever was Roger Crawford's Bad Company. The BRM wheels were the same rims previously used on Tar Babe – check the red centrecaps. (Doug Mische)

Affectionately referred to as "Carlsdirt", Carlsbad Raceway to the north of San Diego regularly played host to VW drag meetings. (Jim Edmiston)

The original Here Comes Da Bug *was destroyed in a roll-over accident in 1972 – as were so many of the early VW quartermilers. Within three weeks, a new car was built to replace it. (Ron Fleming)*

crankcase. They had one major flaw, though, and that was their propensity for breaking rod bolts when subjected to excessive rpm. Many a VW race motor would be effectively sawn in half by the flailing remains of a broken Porsche rod…

Cylinder heads were still based on VW castings, but there was a better understanding of gas flow and a lot of experimentation would be carried out regarding the design of inlet ports, in particular. "Square-port" heads were the flavour of the day among many racers. The Underdog featured a pair of square-port heads created by Gene Berg, and these were used in conjunction with lightweight magnesium manifolds sporting the by-now ubiquitous 48IDA Weber carburettors. Many more parts were starting to become available off the shelf, including equal-length exhaust headers from companies such as S&S, not only a reflection of the growing interest in the VW as an effective weapon in competition, but also in the burgeoning market for performance parts for street-driven cars. There was a greater range of big-bore cylinders on offer, too, with NPR's 92mm kit being particularly popular among the racers.

Another area where there were signs of change was in the field of transmissions, with more racers turning back to using VW-based units in preference to the more expensive Porsche transaxle. This was largely down to the arrival of close-ratio gear sets, produced by Gene Berg, among others, as well as the wider availability of the ZF limited-slip differential. Although the Porsche unit was technically superior, it was far more costly to rebuild in the event of breakage than an equivalent VW gearbox. Many, like Fleming and Gordon, believed that it was worth risking the occasional failure in return for saving money in the long term.

Within months of the *Underdog* hitting the

strips, a new race car came along which set new standards in detailing and overall presentation: the famous *Inch Pincher Too* of Darrell Vittone. This beautifully-prepared roof-chopped 1959 sedan was, in fact, built on the floorpan of the original Inch Pincher. Its *raison d'etre* was that Vittone was tiring of hearing the original car being referred to as "Dean Lowry's old car", for it was Lowry who, while working at EMPI, had been responsible for its transformation from street to race car. The car was a success from the start, and became one of the most feared vehicles in its class (H/Gas).

With its beautifully executed psychedelic paintwork by Molly, and extensive use of cadmium plating on the undercarriage, *Inch Pincher Too* set new standards in the world of VW drag racing. But it is important to realise that most race cars were built for one purpose, and one purpose alone: to go fast. In the majority of cases, presentation came a poor second to improving the performance, and the *Inch*

Pincher Too was the exception that, as the saying goes, proves the rule. Roof-chopping a Beetle is a complex procedure if it is done right – and by "right" we mean in a way that preserves the original profile. It is relatively easy to chop a Beetle in a weekend (and many race cars were), but all too often the roof ends up looking flat.

In the majority of cases, an NHRA-legal four-inch roof chop was carried out solely to exploit the rules to the full, not to win shows. While Metalflake paintwork may have looked cool, in profile the roofs tended to look as if someone had sat on them. The tops of the rear quarter windows lacked the subtle curves of the originals, while the roof panel itself was often flat and featureless, frequently due to the installation of an unsupported Plexiglass insert. The latter was a cheap and easy way to lose weight, and to bypass any problems of panel alignment the chopping process may have caused. Even *Inch Pincher Too* suffered from this…

There were exceptions to the above, though.

A classic photograph that perfectly captures the glory days of VW drag racing. Audley Campbell's Stutt Bee *featured an all-steel roof, while the Anderson Brothers' car used the more popular Plexiglass sunroof insert (Jere Alhadeff/Hot VWs)*

The Anderson Brothers' Here Comes Da Bug, Too *was in many ways the archetypal Gasser. Slighty flared fenders, Plexiglass roof, 'glass decklid and shorty wheelie bars were common features. (Jere Alhadeff/*Hot VWs*)*

*The engine was a Race Shop-built 1950cc unit which allowed the car to run some 50lbs lighter than the original while still remaining legal for the I/Gas class. A beer keg was used as a fuel tank! Note the quality aluminium work. (Jere Alhadeff/*Hot VWs*)*

Take the Anderson Brothers' Gasser, for example. The original *Here Comes Da Bug* had fallen prey to the dreaded, and sadly not at all uncommon, VW high-speed roll-over at the drag strip early in 1972. This was a major blow to the team, as the car had been running quicker and quicker, and looking very much like it was ready to steal the I/Gas class record. After licking their wounds, Rick and Ron Anderson from Culver City, California, decided to build a replacement.

With the help of Mark and Paul Schley (owners of *Lightning Bug*), together with Audley Campbell (*Stutt Bee*), the new car was built in just three weeks! To be strictly accurate, the car – named *Here Comes Da Bug, Too* – wasn't finished until the end of the 1972 season, when it was pulled apart, painted and detailed throughout, but it was a truly Herculean effort to

Full roll-cages became mandatory after some horrific roll-over accidents. Gassers had to run two seats and a "finished" interior – even if that simply meant aluminium panelling.
*(Jere Alhadeff/*Hot VWs*)*

"Aimed by Rick" says the slogan on the door. Rick Anderson was the designated driver of Here Comes Da Bug. Sadly, the car is later thought to have been destroyed in a racing accident in the hands of a new owner.
*(Jere Alhadeff/*Hot VWs*)*

get back into the thick of the Gasser wars so soon after such a major setback.

Starting with a 1961 sunroof sedan bodyshell, the brothers had Casey Collier chop the roof by three-and-three-quarter inches to stay within the NHRA's class-legal maximum chop of four inches. Being a sunroof model obviously helped make the chop a little easier to carry out, especially as a Plexiglass insert was used to fill the remaining hole. In this instance, though, the roof insert was supported by a strengthening rib, which ran across the car just above the driver's head. The roof chop itself was executed with care taken to preserve the lines of the original – and the end result was one of the best-looking Gassers of the early 1970s.

In the quest for weight loss, the fenders, deck lid and hood were all replaced with glassfibre panels supplied by Don Rountree, although the doors remained steel. The fenders were flared to accommodate the wider rear rims and slicks, while the deck lid wore a moulded-in scoop, more for appearance than function. In common with many other cars of the era, the rear fenders and apron were trimmed back to limit the build-up of air under the rear of the vehicle. The completed body was then painted in a dark blue

Roof-chopping was an easy way to improve aerodynamics and reduce weight while staying legal for NHRA Gas-class competition. As-yet unidentified chop-top lines up in the staging lanes at OCIR.
(Ron Fleming)

VW drag racers were well aware of Beetle's handling problems at high-speed. Dennis the Menace sported a small wing under the rear window in an effort to improve stability.
(Ron Fleming)

pearlescent lacquer, with "fogged" detailing, by Eddy Paul, while Steve Feinberg applied the lettering and sponsors' logos. One neat touch at the rear was the push-bar which carried the initials of the Anderson Brothers, a push-bar being a requirement in the Gas classes, even though, by this time in drag racing, most cars were capable of self-starting.

The interior was nicely finished, too – in fact, it was detailed to a higher standard than almost any other VW racer built in the 1970s. The full roll-cage was built by Casey Collier at the Anderson Brothers' request, following the earlier accident. Today, it seems almost unbelievable that a full-on race car such as this wasn't required to carry a roll-cage, but that was, indeed, the case in 1972. The interior itself was panelled out in gold-anodised aluminium sheeting by MCA of Inglewood, CA, with the vestigial dashboard carrying an oil pressure gauge, with a tachometer mounted separately above the dash panel. The seats were glassfibre buckets (two were required to meet class rules) with Naugahyde upholstery by Fitco and equipped with five-point harnesses. The shifter was a Hurst, with the VW handbrake modified to act as a staging brake on the rear wheels.

The bodyshell rested on a VW chassis which

The entry booth at OCIR probably saw more VW Gassers pass through the gate than any other track.
(Roger Grago)

Undoubtedly one of the most beautiful race cars of all time was Greg Aronson's Tar Babe, shown here warming the slicks at OCIR. (Jim Homes)

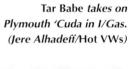

Tar Babe takes on Plymouth 'Cuda in I/Gas. (Jere Alhadeff/Hot VWs)

Tar Babe's interior was partially-trimmed, with carpets on the floor to meet NHRA regulations. (Jere Alhadeff/Hot VWs)

Crossing over from street car to full-on race car, Whit Haydon's Oval-window sedan was a hard-charging J/Gas competitor. (Doug Haydon)

The car was not hacked around like so many race cars as weight was not such an issue in J/Gas. Magnesium American Racing wheels are highly prized today. (Doug Haydon)

had been lightened by replacing the floorpan halves with aluminium sheet. The front suspension was stock VW, rather than the DDS-style tubular front axle favoured by some rivals. The 15in-diameter spun-aluminium wheels were made by ET, and wore Cornwell 5.00x15 tyres at the front and 6.60x15 M&H slicks at the rear. There were no front brakes fitted to the car, with just a pair of stock drums at the rear deemed necessary to bring it to a halt at the end of the quarter-mile. In common with many other VW

Gassers, *Here Comes Da Bug, Too* featured a Porsche transmission, which was supported in a specially-made girdle to prevent the casing from flexing under power. Henry's Axles provided the shafts in the swing-axle rear end, with Traction Master "90-10" shock absorbers used at the front and Gabriel adjustable units at the back.

As the Gas classes were all about weight-per-cubic-inch, the Andersons chose this time around to build a smaller-displacement engine – 1950cc as opposed to the previous 2.0-litre unit.

Steve Tims' Mean Machine Ghia stands in the staging lanes at OCIR. Ghias were never as popular as Beetles for racing despite their slippery shape. (Roger Grago)

This allowed them to build the car some 50lbs lighter than would have been required with the old engine. Race-ready, the chop-top weighed just 1315lbs. The new motor was assembled by Darrell Vittone at the Race Shop in Riverside, and was based around a 78mm Okrasa crankshaft, modified VW "311" con-rods, and a set of 89mm Mahle pistons in bored-out EMPI 88mm cylinders. The camshaft was an Engle F-32 grind, with EMPI lifters and Norris pushrods.

The cylinder heads were reworked VW dual-port casting fitted with EMPI 40mm inlet and 35.5mm exhaust valves opened via EMPI 1.4:1 rocker assemblies. Ported and polished by the Race Shop, the 12.5:1 compression ratio heads were matched to a pair of EMPI manifolds equipped with dual 48IDA Weber carburettors. With the ignition handled by a Joe Hunt-modified Vertex magneto and the exhaust system provided by Four-Tuned, the engine produced 175bhp, some 5bhp down on the old engine, although that was of little consequence bearing in mind the car's lighter weight.

This specification allowed *Here Comes Da Bug, Too* to run the quarter-mile in 11.73 seconds at its first meeting, some 0.35 seconds quicker than the old car and sufficient to establish a new I/Gas record. Later runs saw the car trip the timing clocks in just 11.50 seconds at 114.02mph, making it one of the fastest VW Gassers of all time.

So, what happened to all these Gassers from the 1960s and '70s? Considering how crudely many of them were built, it should come as no surprise that the majority either crashed, or were dismantled for their drive-trains and scrapped. Others were sold to new owners and simply disappeared – several race cars are known to have ended up in Mexico, only to disappear without trace – or, in the case of two famous examples, somehow survived to fight another day. Both *Lightning Bug* and *Tar Babe* managed to survive, if not entirely unscathed. But how many more will appear out of the woodwork in years to come remains to be seen…

Bob McLure was among the first to run a turbocharged motor in a sedan. Little Leroy ran low-10 second times at over 130mph. (Ron Fleming)

Chapter 11

THE CALIFORNIA LOOK LEGACY

*"Where would we be today
had it not been for the pioneers
back in the 1960s and '70s?"*

*Left to right: Gary Berg,
Bill Schwimmer, Dave
Rhoads, Jim Lowe,
Hector Bonilla and Dave
Mason – the photoshoot
that reawakened interest
in the BRM wheel…
(Dean Kirsten/Hot VWs)*

Looking back over the three decades, from the 1960s to the beginning of the '90s, it's possible to see an evolution of almost Darwinian proportions taking place within the Volkswagen scene. In the beginning, there were no hot street cars cruising the streets of Orange County, and no Beetles terrorising the drag strips of California. But then somebody – and that's most likely to have been a "somebody" like Dean Lowry or Darrell Vittone – decided that they could make a Volkswagen go faster than it should.

To begin with, the evolution began with a simple transformation from stocker to something slightly more interesting, courtesy of perhaps little more than a change of exhaust or carbu-

Left to right: Gary Berg, Bill Schwimmer, Dave Rhoads, Jim Lowe, Hector Bonilla and Dave Mason – the photoshoot that reawakened interest in the BRM wheel… (Dean Kirsten/Hot VWs)

The European Bug-In at Chimay in Belgium has captured the spirit of the original SoCal events, attracting particpants from around the globe. Takashi Komori's original "Japanese Looker" sits alongside the former Keith Goss top-chop, Best of Show winner at Bug-In 16. (Author)

If ever proof was needed that the California VW scene is alive and well, you only have to attend one of the many events that take place in and around Orange County, or at tracks like Irwindale and Fontana. (Stephan Szantai)

Steve Beecher on the road. (Stephan Szantai)

DKP spreading the gospel at a classic car meeting. (Author)

rettor. Then the suspension was upgraded to improve the handling, the brakes swapped for, maybe, some redundant Porsche 356 drums and, guess what? Suddenly you found yourself with a car that could run with the big boys.

Had drag racing not been such a massively popular sport in the USA, it's quite possible that we would never have seen anything like a California Look sedan – ever. That's a sobering thought, but think about it: had road racing been as popular in California as it is in Europe, then Lowry and Vittone might have concentrated their efforts on building a Volkswagen with Porsche-like performance characteristics. Perhaps something akin to what we know today as "German Look". But drag racing was the number one motorsport in California (and, indeed, across much of the USA), so it seemed only natural that the VW performance market would expand in that direction.

The 1980s were undoubtedly a time of change, as anyone who visited a Volkswagen show back then will concur. Almost overnight, it seemed that the ever-popular India Red, white or tan hues of the '70s were being replaced by pastel shades, with graphics and even small murals becoming commonplace. What were once no-frills "racers on the street" adopted, save for a number of notable exceptions, something of a more "custom" appearance. In fact,

visitors to popular shows, such as the California VW Jamboree or Small Car Specialties Show-down, in the latter part of the 1980s would have been welcomed by rows of graphic-striped VWs, with the more traditional California Look sedans tucked away – if they were even in attendance. But there was a "secret army" working behind the scenes, members of which wished to turn the clock back to times when the more traditional "Looker" was king.

Chief among them was a trio of Orange County-based enthusiasts, Bill Schwimmer, Greg Brinton and Dave Mason. Together they owned fast street cars in the tradition of the classic hot VWs of the original Der Kleiner Panzers, and it was to founder members of this club that they turned for approval to resurrect the famous DKP name. Almost two decades later, this third generation of the Panzers is now one of the world's most famous and highly respected VW clubs, membership of which is still only by invitation and dependent not only on ownership of the "right" style of car but also the owner having the "right" attitude. There's more to being a DKP

member than simply driving a VW and paying your dues (of which there are none…), as is the case with many clubs.

This resurgence of enthusiasm has spread like wildfire throughout the Volkswagen scene, not only in California, but across the USA, over the

Frank Fabozzi still owns and shows his '80s-built Oval while Dave Mason (below) continues to drive his Bug hard and fast… (Stephan Szantai)

One of a number of cars which raised the bar in terms of attention to detail in the late 1990s and early 2000s was Randy Gates' Split-window sedan. (Staphan Szantai)

Atlantic to Europe and across the Pacific to Japan – and even Thailand. Yes, today there is a thriving California-style VW scene in Bangkok! The spirit of the California look has been kept alive by the media, too, with magazines in Europe and Japan helping to spread the Gospel to a new, younger audience, with the result that the California Look is, almost 40 years since it first came into being, still the dominant style across the globe.

There have been off-shoots of the "Look", too, with Resto-Cal being especially popular – although purists may dispute its origins. A style where performance takes second place to stance (and a plethora of accessories) Resto-Cal is for those who like to take life in the slow lane. In the

Gates' engine featured modern fuel-injection and an MSD ignition system, yet still had the functional beauty of a traditional Weber-carbed, magneto-equipped motor. (Stephan Szantai)

To prove that old show cars never fade away, let alone die, Peaches 'n' Scream *resurfaced in 2007 and is enjoying a new life on the show circuit 20 years after it was built.*
(Stephan Szantai)

magazines and on the Internet forums, you will find many references also to "Old school", a term frequently used to describe a California Look sedan that is, in truth, far removed from what is generally considered to be the archetypal dechromed, stripped-down Looker of old. "Old School" VWs generally retain their factory trim and full interiors, but beneath their near-stock exterior lies (or should lie…) a full-on high-performance drive train – at least they have feature that in common with the seminal Lookers of the early 1970s.

One area in which there has been a marked growth is the super-detailed show-quality Cal Lookers that began to appear in the late 1990s and early years of the 21st century. Cars such as

Paul Bate from the UK owns and built what is without doubt one of the nicest Cal Lookers in modern times. Despite its 10-second potential, the car is still driven regularly on the street.
(Author)

VW rallies may not be as popular as they once were, but clubs like DKP still organise the occasional event. (Stephan Szantai)

Manuel (Tiger) Valasquez's blue 1960 Bug is powered by a 200+bhp 2276cc motor with 11.5:1 compression… (Stephan Szantai)

Doug Mische's *Wocket* (a reference to the licence plate) and Randy Gates' Split-window sedan have spawned a new generation of exceptionally-engineered cars which combine V8-destroying performance with a level of construction that would leave many a show judge speechless.

Mische's car, a 1967 sunroof Beetle, set the standard by which virtually all subsequent new cars have been judged. The owner, a design engineer by trade, took it upon himself to use, for example, CAD-CAM technology to design various details of the car, such as the throttle linkage. And if he wasn't happy with the results first time, he would do it again – and then again, if necessary.

The floorpan of the *Wocket* was repaired and powder-coated twice – leading to Mische earning the nickname of "The Crazy Pan Guy" – the bodyshell was also painted twice, first in the original factory pale blue, then in a vibrant Ferrari red. The 2387cc engine was built (and rebuilt) using the finest components, such as Jet

titanium con-rods, a lightweight Scat crankshaft and a full Mallory ignition system which, incidentally, replaced the original Vertex magneto set-up. Mische's quest for perfection saw the leather-trimmed factory seats being replaced within months by similarly-trimmed aftermarket sports seats, while there was soon talk of new wheels, gauges, shifter... The author once described Doug Mische, much to his delight, as a person in search of solutions to problems that others didn't even know existed. Like the Knights Templars' quest for the Holy Grail, it would appear that Doug Mische's search for the perfect California Look Volkswagen has no end.

Perhaps the most significant influence on the scene in recent years, though, has been the popularity of the Internet forum. Here lies technology which allows images and information to be relayed around the world at the click of a computer mouse. Stories that might have taken months, or even years, to spread throughout the scene can now be enjoyed in an instant. Forums such as the original Cal-Look.com and, later, the

Bill Schwimmer's Coral Red 1959 ragtop runs a Nardi "signature" steering wheel and Berg five-speed transmission. (Author)

DKP line-up at Nick's Burger joint on Orangethorpe in Orange County, headed by Henry Oelker's 1966 sedan. (Stephan Szantai)

Arnie Mohlman of DKP built his 1967 sedan almost 40 years ago. Today it's owned by Russell Ritchie in Scotland. (Author)

Art Alvarez proudly shows off his prized collection of original DKP hood badges and his old club jacket. (Author)

Ron Fleming (seated) and John Lazenby share memories of their times together in the first generation DKP in the '60s. (Author)

Jim Holmes and Dean Kirsten (right), both still actively involved with the scene over 30 years down the road… (Author)

Taylor Walton's Sea Blue '65 sedan was the talking point of the DKP Pre-Classic cruise night in June 2008. The car looks oh-so traditional yet features a lot of neat detailing and modern touches, such as the crank-fired ignition system, for example. (Stephan Szantai)

Ghias are still not as popular in the scene, and probably never will be. However, Mike Lawless' coupé still flies the flag on the strip. (Stephan Szantai)

Norwegian Cal Look Lounge, have done much to educate and enthuse, relaying technical information or photographs of long-lost race cars to an audience hungry to learn all it can about how to make a fast VW live, or what it was really like in "the old days". And it is important to bear in mind where would we be today had it not been for the pioneers back in the 1960s and '70s?

Today, it is also far easier to buy high-performance parts for an air-cooled Volkswagen, long after the VW factory ceased building such a car. Parts are readily available in most countries through specialist shops or, failing that, by mail order over the Internet. Indeed, it has often been

Der RennKäfer Cup was conceived as a show and go points series, with points being awarded in a car show and for performance on the drag strip. DRKC spawned a generation of ultra-fast street-legal sedans, such as Rich Dickinson's '67. (Stephan Szantai)

Nick's Burgers used to be called Dairy Queen and has hosted DKP cruise nights for many years. (Author)

said that all you need today to build a 12-second Volkswagen is a credit card and a computer with Internet access. While that may not be entirely true, for you still need to know how to assemble the parts correctly (and how to chose the right parts in the first place), there is undoubtedly a far wider selection of quality components available today than there has ever been.

There has been a regeneration of the event scene, too, with the return of the original California-based Bug-In, and its Belgian-based offshoot, European Bug-In, providing a focus for enthusiasts on both sides of the Atlantic Ocean. For as long as environmental legislation allows us to have fun with our cars, the future for such events looks very bright indeed.

The California Look has come a long way since the days when fitting a velocity stack to a stock carburettor, bolting on a custom-made glasspack muffler and installing a set of chrome reversed-rim wheels was the height of SoCal cool. But, as I hope has been demonstrated by this book, there is a bloodline which has remained unbroken for over four decades – a bloodline created out of enthusiasts' obsession with turning the humble People's Car into a muscle car owner's worst nightmare.

Magnetos and 48IDAs may be making way for ECUs and fuel-injection, but the thrill of leaving a Corvette (or Honda, or Porsche) for dead at the stoplight will live on forever.

If you need evidence of the strength of Caifornia Look today, you need look no further than this line-up of 48IDA-equipped machinery... (Stephan Szantai)

From left to right: Doug Haydon, Mike Hunsaker, John Lazenby, Ron (FAT) Fleming, Doug Mische and Rich (Bug-In) Kimball. Still having fun after all these years. (Author)

DKP

The legend lives on. Members of all three generations of the best-known California Look VW club in the world assembled at VW Classic for a once in a lifetime photo. Now let the party begin…

Der Kleiner Panzers